THE BUTTERFLY EFFECT

An anthology of stories by inspirational
women impacting the world

Groundbreaking, life-changing global solutions are provided in these pages. Demonstrating how one person can change the world. By using passion and purpose, love, intuition, sacred methods, or sheer determination and grit.

If you are looking for inspiration and guidance, ways to enhance your personal journey or make your mark on the world this book is a must-read!

Serena Scarlett
International award-winning author, editor, therapeutic counsellor and mentor

Disclaimer:
The authors in this book do not dispense medical advice or prescribe the use of any technique as a form of treatment for physical, emotional, or medical problems without the advice of a physician, either directly or indirectly. The intent of the authors is only to offer information of general nature to help you on your quest for emotional, physical, and spiritual well-being. In the event the readers use any of the information in this book for themselves, the authors and the publisher assume no responsibility for their actions.

CONTENTS

DEDICATION

To the magnificent women of the world, who embody grace, strength and unwavering faith.

To the fearless, unstoppable, and radiant women of the world, who spread their wings and stir the winds of change with grace, courage and strength.

To you, the brilliant butterflies who flit and flutter, spreading light and beauty wherever you go, this is a testament to the transformative power of your courage, passion and determination.

This anthology is dedicated to you, the brilliant butterflies who spread beauty, hope and inspiration with every flutter of your wings. Your passion, resilience and unwavering spirit have created ripples of positive change, resulting in a butterfly effect that has touched lives far and wide.

Your strength, wisdom and determination serve as a shining beacon of light, guiding others to reach for the stars and soar towards their dreams.

May this anthology serve as a reminder of the limitless possibilities that can be achieved when you let your spirit soar and follow your dreams.

This is a celebration of you, the women who inspire and uplift, leaving a positive impact in the world, and making the world a more vibrant and colorful place, one flap of your wings at a time.

ACKNOWLEDGEMENTS

The creation of this anthology would not have been possible without the unwavering support, encouragement and love of the many people who stood by me every step of the way.

With a heart overflowing with gratitude, first, I dedicate this acknowledgement to God Almighty, and to the cast of characters who made this anthology possible.

To my beautiful daughter, Ayomide Oluwole, your caring heart, love, selfless spirit and giving heart is beyond measure. Thank you for being a constant source of light in my life, and the voice of reasoning, and love you to bits.

To my beloved son, Ayotunde Oluwole, who has been my advisor, cheerleader, and constant source of inspiration. Your unwavering love and care have been the fuel that keeps me moving forward. I love you to the moon and back.

To my beautiful daughter, Ayokunle, our chats provided the colors that brighten my days of darkness, and love you with my heart.

To the amazing and beautiful women in my corner of life; Janis F. Kearney, Tarja Wiklund, Valerie Fox, Samantha Louise, Nicole S. Mason and Cathy Derksen, thank you for cheering me on, your unwavering support and prayers. Your encouragement has been a beacon in the darkness, guiding me towards the light of creativity.

I am eternally grateful to the awesome Krystal Hille and her phenomenal team for their outstanding publishing support. Your dedication to the vision of this anthology has been awe-inspiring.

My heartfelt thanks go to Ambassador Adeyinka Asekun and Sandra Yeung-Racco for accepting to write a Goodwill Message and the Foreword of this book. To the leadership at Obafemi Awolowo University, Ile Ife, Nigeria, my alma mater; Prof. A. S. Bamire, Vice Chancellor, and Prof. Akanni Akinyemi,

Executive Director of the Central Office of Research, thank you for the honor of the book presentation.

My deepest gratitude goes to my brother, Muyiwa Osinowo, for his guidance, wisdom and support through thick and thin.

To the collaborative authors who accepted to be part of the vision and anthology, and who stood through to the end, I am forever grateful.

Frank Auddino, your mentorship and guidance have been invaluable, and I appreciate your support.

Ron Hogue, how can I forget the several virtual meetings and chats, discussing this vision, and your unflinching support, advice, and guidance. You're a gift to humanity and I appreciate you immensely.

Paula Talman of Shawmind UK, as the not-for-profit partner on mental health advocacy, your enthusiasm and willingness to collaborate on this project is a testament of your large and kind heart.

Finally, to my creative team, Segun Oni, Ayobami Oke, and John Oladele, your creativity is superbly acknowledged and appreciated. Thank you for sticking with me through the rigorous design process. Sunday and Tunmise Akinola, thank you for your love and care through the years, thick and thin. To Olugbenga Adewinle, your bodacious spirit and large heart, as well as resourcefulness are worthy of emulation and appreciated.

To my friends who had my back and shared their love, care, and resources, I see you, and thank you for being true to friendship; Toyo Idris, Bunmi Omotesho, Olakunle Osobu, Kayode Daramola, Joke Benson, Kemi Ayeni, Debo Adeosun, and Bet Basnet.

To Olugbenga Adewoye, my brother from another mother, for your unflinching support, love, indefatigable spirit, and prayers when all hell broke loose, I am eternally grateful, and love you to the moon and back.

This anthology is a testament to the power of love, care, and unwavering support. May the words within its pages continue to inspire and empower women globally, as we all make our own butterfly effect in this world.

I am eternally grateful to each and every one of you for being a part of this journey and for helping bring *The Butterfly Effect Anthology* to life.

And to God Almighty, for giving me the creativity, time, resources, wisdom, and opportunity, I give thanks and praise.

Thank you all,

Oluneye Oluwole®

March   2023

FOREWORD

MESSAGE FROM FORMER COUNCILOR

SANDRA YEUNG-RACCO

It gives me great pleasure to extend my warmest congratulations to Oluneye Oluwole, founder of *Story Chest Group Inc.,* on bringing forward the initiative of compiling an anthology of stories from women across the globe, entitled *"The Butterfly Effect: Women Impacting the World."*

The objective of *"The Butterfly Effect"* anthology is to bring about a collection of stories, memories, and experiences that will help inspire girls and women worldwide by illustrating their ideas, passion and vision, promoting gender equality, empowering women, and leading to progressive transformation. These stories will embrace the concept of inclusivity within diversity, demonstrating that a path to peace and equality is possible and confirming that the stories we write today can inspire future generations of women for years to come.

As a public servant with a music degree behind me, I am a firm believer that the Arts play an integral role in shaping the character of any community. Through the Arts, we can keep history alive, offer outlets for social commentary and encourage education through creativity. Creative projects, such as this anthology, reach out not only to those within our own community, but across the nation, continents and world, by encouraging honest and thought-provoking discussions that will help build stronger and more inclusive communities for all.

Thank you Oluneye and all the women who have contributed their personal reflections to this engaging and important anthology collection. May it inspire us all to reflect on our own stories and journeys that will help create a positive impact on our communities and each other.

Let us stand together to support and work with each other to make our world a better place for everyone, now and into the future!

Sincerely yours,

Sandra Yeung-Racco, B. Mus.Ed., A.R.C.T.
楊 士 淳
President, Empowering Your Vision
Former Councillor, City of Vaughan

ENDORSEMENT

A GOODWILL MESSAGE FROM THE HIGH COMMISSIONER OF NIGERIA TO CANADA, HIS EXCELLENCY ADEYINKA ASEKUN, ON THE OCCASION OF THE LAUNCH OF THE BUTTERFLY EFFECT—WOMEN IMPACTING THE WORLD, AN ANTHOLOGY OF STORIES OF TWENTY GLOBAL WOMEN LEADERS, COMPILED BY OLUNEYE OLUWOLE

I am delighted to join people worldwide in celebrating the efforts of Oluneye Oluwole, a Nigerian immigrant woman entrepreneur in Canada and the Founder/CEO of Story Chest Group Inc. Canada.

Her idea of convening an anthology of stories by women from various backgrounds to inspire more women entrepreneurs worldwide is commendable. The goal is in tandem with the ideals of citizen diplomacy, a cardinal aim of the foreign policy of the Nigerian government, which includes but is not limited to encouraging Nigerians across the globe to engage with the rest of the world in a meaningful, mutually beneficial dialogue about the essence of humanity.

I am also supportive of the goal of the anthology aligning with the UN Sustainable Development Goals (5) – *"Achieve Gender Equality and Empower All Women and Girls" by 2030.*

Empowering women through literacy and education allows the family to make strategic life choices that invariably affect society. Women are the primary custodians of children and the elderly worldwide. Therefore, they take the lead in aiding families in adjusting to the challenges and realities of our time.

The Butterfly Effect—Women Impacting the World will significantly affect the lives of many women, and humanity worldwide, to ignite positive change.

Change often takes place when we read about the personal narratives of resilience. However, unpacking the journeys of these global leaders by Oluneye indicates that building confidence and rising above challenges is not a one-size-fits-all affair, as these journeys are unique to each person's identity. So, as you read these experiences, may you find hope as you adapt to adversity to make an impact in your locality, and may the stories ignite your passion for rising above all obstacles in life.

I commend the curator and lead author, Oluneye Oluwole, for compiling such edifying works creatively to inspire more women. I also congratulate all the women who shared these inspirational stories. Indeed, you have created a "butterfly effect" for an enduring legacy.

H.E. Adeyinka Asekun
High Commissioner of the Federal Republic of Nigeria to Canada

NON-PROFIT SUPPORT

A WORD FROM THE CEO: SHAWMIND UK, A MENTAL HEALTH NON-PROFIT ORGANISATION

We are extremely grateful for the connection with this book and wish to thank Oluneye Oluwole for her kind support. We wish to take a moment to share with you how the money you have spent on this book is going to be utilised to support the mental health of future generations.

Since its founding in 2016, Shawmind has been committed to ensuring that children and young people's mental fitness is improved. In 2017, we raised signatures to force a parliamentary debate on children's mental health that has led to mental health education becoming compulsory in schools. We continued to pursue the importance of this and make it the core mission as a charity.

Since the pandemic, children and young peoples' mental health has worsened considerably. A report recently published shows that almost two million of England's nine million children are missing school regularly. Hospital admissions for eating disorders increased by over 80% during the pandemic, and we are increasingly finding school refusals and massive increases in anxiety levels among children and young people in the schools we serve.

Mental health and poor mental fitness in those under the age of 18 is in crisis and we are committed to change the trajectory many of the young people are on and support them with the struggles they face.

Our approach is simple but paramount to revolutionizing mental health in the UK. We provide early intervention care, support, training and guidance before our children and young people hit crisis or breaking point. By addressing the problems before they arise or very early on, we can ensure children and young people are equipped with the right strategies, information, and emotional support to navigate their issues early on, thus reducing the risk of the situation becoming worse.

Apart from supporting children and young people, we also support parents and teachers with important training on how to manage a child or young person's mental health through our unique and bespoke program, Headucation.

Our Headucation Programme is a mental fitness education package for schools, which helps us bring about a transformation in the mental health of the next generation: working with local educational authorities and partner organizations we are bringing a whole-school approach to mental health, helping schools to develop a culture shift towards sustainable, better mental health and wellbeing for all.

As a charity, Shawmind relies on our communities and organisations to help us raise the funds we need to be able to continue with this vital work, which we provide to schools as a fully funded educational resource and training package.

There are many ways in which people can get involved with our work. Running your own event, taking part in a challenge, booking one of our training courses and of course, by purchasing this book.

It costs us approximately £6 to support a child and £3000 to provide resources and training to a school for a year, meaning that every penny fundraised for us really does go straight towards changing the lives of children and young people around the UK.

The funds from this book will make a difference to change or perhaps even save the life of a child or young person, by allowing them access to the right support when they need it most.

With deep appreciation,

Peter Wingrove
Shawmind   CEO

INTRODUCTION

"Butterflies are like women—we may look prettier and delicate, but baby, we can fly through a hurricane."

– Betty White

*O*ur world as we knew it was so drastically disrupted in 2020 by a pandemic that, today, it has become a place of uncertainty, fear, worry, pain, injustice, bias, hunger, and famine.

The COVID-19 pandemic impacted our lives extensively, with women being more adversely affected economically, socially, and mentally. It revealed underlying prejudices within our societies, especially against women in the workplace, at home, and in communities.

Conversely, it was also a period where women from every corner in the world not only found, but amplified their voices as they also discovered their self confidence and creative elements to start new businesses.

Despite this, the number of women who challenged the status quo and changed their narratives remains significantly low when compared to hundreds of millions across the world whose lives have been thrown curve balls, especially during the pandemic. These women remain unseen, unheard, and underrepresented.

Not immune to life's curve balls, I had my fair share of pandemic woes. During the summer of 2020, my world was shattered with personal losses of different shades and color—a divorce embodied by grief, hurt, betrayal, and pain. A year on, (just when I thought a rainbow was in view), I found myself dealing with the loss of my immediate younger sister after her eleven-year battle with cancer. She died the day after my birthday.

1

The metamorphosis of my life's events began in the cold, dark, gloomy days, weeks, and months of this period and, through reflection on past events, resulted in the emergence of a butterfly. During my darkest days, I found strength in my vulnerable state to see the rainbow in the storm, which we are often blind to when life deals us a bad card.

As women and natural nurturers, we incubate stories of our lived experiences, yet mental screens such as Imposter Syndrome, stigmas, and negative perceptions about ourselves hinder us from taking ownership of our stories. We question ourselves, asking, *"What makes you qualified? How dare you do that?"*. This prevents us from seeing the gems in our stories and turning them to superpowers. They stop us from celebrating our authenticity and vulnerability and taking what we own and know to the next level.

Our world is constantly being ravaged by wars, famine, and pandemic outbreaks, and the population of women who are negatively impacted is on the increase. So there's no better time than now to support them to build their confidence and inspire them to develop their creativity and abilities, and to write their stories.

I evolved into a butterfly through the metamorphosis of the life events and struggles I endured. I resurrected as a symbol of endurance, change, hope, and life.

Therefore, my mission to humanity and women most especially, is to find "butterflies" like me, who have "flown through the hurricane", then bring them together and into the lives of other women across the world. To help them discover who they are and their deepest life's purpose.

The Butterfly Effect, an anthology of stories written by female thought leaders, is about waking up the sleeping giant and greatness in women of all races, color, and age across the world. It centers on inspiring women to make an impact in their communities through their stories, creativity, passion, and talents. It's very much about creating an enduring legacy and culture of tenacity, resilience, and sustainability for future generations.

The vision is that this anthology of women's stories will be a spark that ignites the fire in women around the world; that it creates a reverberating *Butterfly Effect* across cities, countries, and continents. It is my desire that it inspires them to make an impact in their communities with their passion, creativity, and talents.

In the words of Mother Teresa, *"I alone cannot change the world, but I can cast a stone across the waters to create many ripples."* In the same vein, it is my dream that *The Butterfly Effect* will create many ripples globally, for women and our communities.

Thank you for being part of this great vision.

Oluneye Oluwole®

President and Founder, Story Chest Group Inc., Canada

Executive Producer and Host, Storytellers With Oluneyespeaks

March   2023

PART I

OVERCOMING ADVERSITY

OLUNEYE OLUWOLE

YES, TO OPEN DOORS

"Be prepared to seize the opportunity when it comes your way

~ Christine Lagarde

I was born in the ancient city of Ibadan, south-western Nigeria, with big curious eyes. I have always been the girl with big, wide, and piercing eyes. These eyes have not stopped darting back and forth with curiosity. Curious about my environment, curious about what the world is all about. Simply curious about anything and everything. Wanting to see more and know more. Aside from my eyes, I've always been independent and adventurous. I enjoyed my environment. The outdoors was my playground, creative space, and freezone. I was in my element when I could freely explore the world around me.

My name – *Oluneye* has an uncommon, not-so-feminine ring and uniqueness I loathed for a better part of my life. This was due to endless teasing from friends in school and around. Who names their daughter *Oluneye*? I questioned my parents about my name. My father consoled me with the fact that I was named after his great-grandmother – Efunneye! This was neither comforting, nor acceptable to me. It further plunged me into a state of unease. I experienced discomfort whenever I introduced myself.

One time in my mid-30s, I introduced myself to a client. He squealed with excitement. He let me know the rarity, beauty, and uniqueness of my name. Saying that he'd only known a male with my name, had never met a female with that name in his entire life, and this was a first, heartwarming and rare opportunity for him.

It was the moment of an epiphany for me. That my unusual, uncommon, and unfeminine name stems from being special, beautiful, talented, and a rare gift to the world. From then on, I wore my name like a badge. I stood taller, with my shoulders squared, trusting in what the future held for me. With new confidence I looked forward to what opportunities life would offer me.

I was pleased to be described as bodacious, confident, independent-minded, adventurous, and unconventionally feminine.

My journey in life became one embedded with different phases and moments, all geared towards building the person I have become today. This self-actualization was because I said yes.

First Yes

My curiosity launched me into the world of entrepreneurship. This quest began at a time when I least expected it. It was borne out of necessity – a mompreneur with three children, all under ten years of age!

It began in October 1997, when I had a newborn with no job and two other young children.

An opportunity for a career in travel and tourism presented itself, and I acted on the words of Sir Richard Branson, - *"If somebody offers you an amazing opportunity but you are not sure you can do it, say yes – then learn how to do it later!"* I said yes! Despite my initial lack of industry knowledge and experience, I immersed myself and upskilled. By utilising every available resource, I became a sought-after reservations and ticketing officer.

But in a twist of fate, due to the toxic work environment, a fallout from that job brought me to a crossroad and pivotal career moment. – I had to job hunt again or become an entrepreneur. I opted for the not-so-easy road of entrepreneurship, and baptism into the crazy, chaotic, and uncertain world of entrepreneurs, innovators, and dreamers.

My first bodacious desire and passion was to be a tourism entrepreneur, to document the history of my home country – Nigeria. This was a venture my father considered to be humongous to take on single-handedly and well out of my league. Undeterred, and unrelenting, I journeyed on in my passion, and in the last quarter of 2003, the inspiration to write my first book, was birthed – *'My Heritage, The History of Ogun State'*. I completed this three-part documentation of the history, heritage and of the people, places, and culture of my native State in 2006.

I encountered several hurdles from within and without – lack of financial support, gender-based, cultural, and patriarchal biases, as well as the challenges involved in independent publishing, marketing, and distribution.

Second Yes

In yet another twist of fate, after plunging myself into the documentation for my first book, I was part of an economic summit in my native State – Ogun State. During the summit, in October 2003, I shared my findings. I presented my observations, opinions and opportunities in tourism for Ogun State, which stemmed from my experience in the field and for the documentation of my book. Subsequently I was offered a leadership opportunity in 2004, as a member of the Board of Tourism in my State - a role I served for the next three years.

Third Yes

In 2007, at the end of my first leadership appointment, I had a meeting with the former Governor of my State. The bodacious, confident, independent-minded, adventurous, and unconventionally feminine 'me' met with the governor and other political stalwarts, to discuss the launch of my book. It was presented to the State, at an official occasion. I didn't want an ordinary book launch. Why? I guess I had never been comfortable with the 'ordinary'. Why not raise the bar higher and make it a state government affair, giving the book its due worth. It involved immense stress, near-death experiences as well as a lot of fun and adventure.

Unbeknownst to me, from this meeting, another opportunity lurked in the background. Unexpectedly, I was offered another leadership opportunity – to serve as Supervisory Councillor in my Local Government and State. Saying yes to this opportunity, rocked the boat of my marriage. For three years, I fought battles within and without, from taking on this opportunity. I wish I could say that, I came out unscathed, but like every battle, there were scars.

Fourth Yes

At the expiration of my tenure as a Supervisory Councillor in December 2010, I received a call out of the blue, to yet another opportunity. I was offered a consultancy role for a development and media project, ahead of the 2011 elections in Nigeria.

When this opportunity came knocking, the bodacious, adventurous, me stepped in, and said *yes*! This opportunity involved studio and street interviews within the cities of Lagos and London. This gave birth to the inspiration for my second book – '*Dreams of A Patriot*', a book that examined leadership. It explored the characteristics of leaders from the lens of Nigeria's post-independence of 50 years.

Fifth Yes

Five years on, the desire to document my political journey as a legacy for women, birthed my first memoir in 2015. In that same year I had another opportunity to author a biographical publication – The 'Quintessential Colossus'. I couldn't resist saying yes once again.

Saying Yes

Over two decades, I undertook an independently driven journey. It was a tumultuous time with many challenges, patriarchal and cultural biases. It was devoid of supportive mentoring. There was no safe, enabling entrepreneurial community or network. I took many risks, experienced failures and made mistakes. My entrepreneurial journey, bodacious adventures, and my saying yes opportunities, pitched me against societal expectations as a woman, mother and wife. Gradually and steadily, a concrete brick began its slow, but negative impact on the walls of my marriage.

Knowing that the walls of my marriage had broken irretrievably, I took the opportunity to leave the shores of the country I'd known for most of my life. It was a good time to leave as it was just a matter of time for the ticking bomb to explode. In a patriarchal society, I had pushed the boundaries to its limits. In July 2020, I got divorced by my husband of 30 years.

Unfortunately, the pandemic of 2020 became an entrapment, where my plans, like everyone else's, were upturned. While in the vessel of the pandemic voyage, I pondered on my journey. I wished for an understanding partner who valued my creativity, gifts, and talents. Someone who could understand my purpose, and who I am.

During this period, a different side of me was unveiled. I was thrust into the world of poetry and songs. The days that followed my divorce, though dark and lonely, were the perfect canvas for the unfolding of my gifts in the world of spoken word. My lived experiences and saying yes to open doors, had been preparing me for a much greater door of opportunity and assignment - to become the 'who, what, and how', I was searching for through the years, not only to women around the world, but future generations.

Rear Mirror

Looking through the rear mirror, would I have done it another way? – by saying no to opportunities? I think not!

I ruminate on my meaningful and purposeful life. If I had said no, how *would I have been invited to speak to the Soft Ball Team of Santa Clara University, California, organized by HERricanes Inc. USA, where signed copies of my book, Dreams of A Patriot (2012), were donated to the sportswomen who attended the event in 2022?*

How would I have received a Congressional Recognition Award by Congresswoman Sheila Jackson Lee, U.S. Representative for Texas' 18th congressional district? During the launch of my third book and political memoir – 'Serve With Heart And Might' this honor was granted to me, in recognition of my achievements in entrepreneurship, leadership and mentoring women.

How would I have written a collection of poems, songs and books in 2021, with poetry performances, and numerous song releases?

How would I have birthed 'Storytellers With Oluneyespeaks', in 2021? How could I have created this global community of entrepreneurs, creative innovators, thought-leaders, subject-matter experts and future leaders?

How would this Anthology – 'The Butterfly Effect' be birthed, that features women from all over the world, with fire in their belly to impact their world.

How would a little girl with big, curious eyes from Odogbolu – a small town in Ogun State, southwest Nigeria, have become so incredible: a global thought-leader, impact influencer, congressional recognition award recipient, mentor, serial entrepreneur, international speaker, spoken word poet, songwriter, storyteller, on a global stage.

Throughout the highs and lows, I stayed true to who I am – creative, adventurous, bodacious, intuitive, passionate, resilient, ambitious, relationship-builder and risk-taker, knowing that greatness lies within. I'm still curious to do, know, see, and be more.

I continue with sheer grit, resilience, passion, undaunted faith, courage and I keep weathering the storms, challenges and biases. Yes, I have flown through the hurricanes – adversities, pain, hurt, rejection, betrayal, lack, loss, and loneliness. Do I have scars from these epic challenges and obstacles? Yes, I have scars. But I say yes to being stronger, smarter, wiser, finding myself, finding my voice. Yes, to greater purpose, yes to inspire the woman reading this chapter and book, and yes, to trusting the journey to purpose.

I found a greater purpose through my lived experience – including failures and successes, all of which have become intrinsic assets, messages and platforms of inspiration, encouragement, transformation, and hope to women and everyone around the world.

Today, *OLUNEYESPEAKS WITH ONE MIC, ONE VOICE, ONE STAGE*, to make the world a better place - to inspire many to higher expressions of themselves, and to encourage others to leave footprints of legacy.

It's saying YES TO OPEN DOORS!

Oluneye Oluwole®

President and Founder, Story Chest Group Inc, Canada

Executive Producer and Host, Storytellers With Oluneyespeaks

ABOUT THE AUTHOR

OLUNEYE OLUWOLE®

Oluneye Oluwole® is the Founder of Story Chest Group Inc., Canada, a storytelling, multimedia company, and the Creator of 'Storytellers With Oluneyespeaks', an inspirational, storytelling, networking platform and community for creatives, entrepreneurs, innovators, founders and professionals.

An author of many books, *The Butterfly Effect* is her first anthology of stories, and she writes across diverse genres - leadership, political, historical, biographical, and poetry. She is a storyteller, serial entrepreneur, spoken word poet, keynote speaker, and a subject-matter-expert, with experience across several industries.

Oluneye has an unquenchable energy and passion for storytelling, entrepreneurship, women empowerment, and leadership.

Through the multidisciplinary entrepreneurship development consultancy organization, she founded – African Hub International, Oluneye supports the development of entrepreneurship ecosystems within Africa, with her experience and expertise that span over two decades.

Connect with Oluneye here:

Website: www.oluneyespeaks.com

LinkedIn: https://www.linkedin.com/in/oluneyeoluwole/

Instagram: @oluneyespeaks

LANA IVANOVA

HOW MY HEART STARTED BEATING FOR THE THIRD TIME

*I*magine this. I am a six-year-old girl who last saw her mother one year ago. The day I was to see her after this long period of absence, I went to the airport with my grandmother. A third escort accompanied me which is that of anxiety and anticipation within me. As Mum walked towards us, I ran with all the strength within me to get to her for a long-awaited hug. After the prolonged hug and helping her carry some of the bags, I said to her, "Mummy, mummy, I need to tell you something! I had an operation and my heart stopped and started beating again." She is shocked as she knows nothing about that. Her suitcase falls off her hand with a loud bang. She turned to my grandmother with astonishment and some anger in her voice: "What operation? What does she mean her heart stopped? Mother, what is she saying?"

I was born in Sakha Yakutia, one of the republics in Russia. A land of permanent frost and diamonds, where winter comes for nine months, and the temperatures often fall below -50C. My heart would always beat faster during these times.

As I was staying with my grandparents for one year during that harsh climate, it was discovered that I had a benign tumor which needed surgery. While everything was happening, I was staying with my grandparents who shouldered the burden and had decided not to inform my parents. They

14

believed sparing them was necessary as they were busy and far away from us.

The surgery was a major and serious one and my heart stopped working for a moment during the process. My grandmother suggested there was no need informing my parents since everything went on successfully and I was recovering quickly. Besides, they knew that my parents would be coming over during the summer holidays just a few months away. And out of innocence and happiness, I poured out everything to my mother upon seeing her. She also learned that here, in the town of Illivhevsk, Odesa region in Ukraine, my heart started to beat for the second time.

Growing up, I often returned and spent numerous school and university vacations in Tarea at the Black Sea. I fell in love with a guy who lived there and moved to Odesa to start a new story. A true love story; we have been together for more than twenty years and have two kids.

Many years later, we were already living in Warsaw, Poland, with my small family. And when Russia attacked Ukraine in February 2022, I felt like my heart had stopped again. For a couple of days, I felt like I could not breathe properly. I felt emotional pain inside, multiplied by shame and guilt for everything. With my homeland hurting so many people, for me to be able to keep my everyday life while my dear people in Ukraine were suffering. People of the country where my mother, husband, and children were born.

As many people in Poland and around the world did, we started to help Ukraine immediately. Our usual routine was donating to the Ukrainian and assisting refugees. We helped our families, and friends in getting to Poland and other European countries. We provided them with what they needed; buying food, clothes, and everything we could.

While we collectively did everything we could to help and rescue these displaced and traumatized persons, I wanted to do more. I thought deeply and hardly on how I could genuinely help from my very own personal contributions. Hence, while I earnestly gave my best towards the collective efforts, I also continuously thought of ways to help out. An idea came at last.

As a coach who helps people achieve their goals, hone their public speaking, and speak up in foreign languages, I decided to help in this manner. Thus, as someone from Russia, working with English language with a fluency in Polish and full understanding of Ukrainian languages, I decided to bridge every language barrier that the refugee Ukrainians might face or be facing in their new settlements.

While the focus of personal help has been figured out and settled, there existed another most challenging confrontation; the issue of being judged as a Russian. The country is actually causing and perpetrating this horror and displacement of innocent and helpless lives. This brought doubts, going forth and back, and gave me mixed feelings of what and what ought not be done. It was an inner battle that almost pulled me out of my good plans to help those in need.

After a long inner struggle, I decided to take my chances and see how things unfolded with this plan of mine. As a result of my determined resolution, I decided to write a targeted message on my social media. It read thus:

"English boost for Ukraine!" Imagine that the war is over. The goal is to now look for worldwide opportunities. Imagine a peaceful Ukraine, reconstructed, prospering, and heading to the future. English is a universal language tool that connects people and opens opportunities. This is the launching of the "English-speaking Boost online course. Please fill in the form to register for free."

With this, I quickly gathered a decent group of people eager to boost their speaking and language skills in this situation which were mostly women. These were women with kids who left the country because of the war and stayed in various countries of Europe, waiting for the fight to end. And naturally many had not even been thinking about the future.

I had participants joining sessions from many countries, including Ukraine, Romania, Croatia, Poland, France, Germany, Ireland, Latvia, and Estonia. This was a group that had a stunning level of professionalism and expertise. I saw these women who had stopped their previous lives and reinvented their lives. They were living in new places with an uncertain future, and I could not help but admire them.

Two of my friends voluntarily joined me to moderate the course. One of them was Florian, my fantastic partner in crime who is an inspirational Toastmaster and a public speaking master from London. And the second one was Demelza, a small talk queen devoted to literature, movies, music, with a love of cuisine. She is from Santa Barbara, California, US. Iryna, a professional from the tech industry, originally from Ukraine, living in Mannheim, Germany now, contributed even though we were not acquainted before.

Here we were, connecting people from Santa Barbara through Mannheim and London to Warsaw, gathering mesmerizing stories from our participants along the way. It was a fantastic feeling to know I was not doing it alone. Our participants cherished the sessions with Florian and Demelza, practicing their speaking skills and adjusting their accents.

I was bringing new tools for language classes every week, but the brightest moments happened at our speaking sessions. One could hear us talking about books and movies, electric cars, personal experiences, job interviews and career opportunities. We shared stories about our business trips, different countries' peculiarities and traditions, and our personal motivations. We discussed how to cook our favorite dishes and bake bread, spoke about how we like to treat ourselves, and practiced all the possible small talk.

As the sessions progressed, there were evident improvements among the participants. I can vividly remember our participants' final presentations when they felt confident enough to speak on topics they were eager to share. Rada told us about her journey with social dancing. Olena made us dream about traveling again. Teasing us with her ability to fly through life and dare to live freely. Tetiana revealed her path as an interior designer, inviting us to a beautiful world of style. Alina pumped up our energy and made us think about happiness. Alena introduced a fabulous palette of online educational opportunities for the development of many potential skills.

Every boosting session was unique, yet I know one thing that could unite them all. They were full of moments of togetherness, support, smiles, and inspiration. With smatterings of, some English boosting along the way. Finally, I felt I was able to breathe fully. And here was how my heart started to beat for the third time.

In a future where Ukraine has emerged victorious from the war, I wanted the country to become a prospering and internationally connected nation. In this image, the main wish I had was that many people in Ukraine could speak English at a reasonable level. The English language is the most well used language in international communication. I know the future is not coming in a snap of time and I see my English boost project as a small step towards this future image.

We often have little control over significant outside events and circumstances. The war may be one of them. However, we can always control our actions and reactions to those events. In my own case, I was devastated but gave my best. I was drawn to and focused on what I could manage rather than worrying about things outside my control. I took a proactive approach, launched the boost, brought value, and did my best with the situation.

Yes, my journey in life has given me the chance for my heart to start beating at three key instances. However, it was one instance in particular that directly affected me the most. It was when I got that sweeping realization of my deepest heart's desire. It was when I heard a call to action and I pursued it with the English Boost online classes.

When my heart started beating, that third time was the best one for me. I could see fulfillment and lives liberated and a new beginning amidst when all had appeared to have been lost. Keep heart, never lose hope.

ABOUT THE AUTHOR

LANA IVANOVA

LANA IVANOVA is a communication coach, business trainer, TEDx speakers' mentor, and "Tell Your Story" Speaking Club Creator.

After leaving the organizational consulting sphere, she now helps people find their unique communication style and express themselves openly.

Lana's primary goal is to support non-natives of different ways of life to speak up in English and tell their own stories. She is a long-time member of Toastmasters International and a few times President of Poland's First Toastmasters club in Warsaw, Poland. Lana is a wife and mother of two kids, half Russian and half Ukrainian, born in the Republic of Sakha Yakutia, Russia. She has lived with her family in Ukraine for ten years, just before the hybrid part of the Russo-Ukrainian war started in 2014. She is now living her third life in Warsaw, Poland.

Lana believes in the power of lightness and small continuous change. This approach transformed her from a shy girl from the frozen edge of the world, to the international public speaking contests- and conferences participant and a coach who unmutes people.

Connect with Lana here:

https://www.instagram.com/lana.iva.nova/

https://www.linkedin.com/in/lana-ivanova-6201079

https://linktr.ee/lana.ivanova

TARJA WIKLUND

LEGACY OF GENERATIONS

$\mathscr{A}$s a child I watched my grandmother knitting in dim light, her face leaning over to watch the stocking sticks move in a rhythmic movement, loop by loop, layer by layer. Her face was focused, determined and calm, her eyes sparkled and expressed the Universe in its whole. I sat at the couch and watched her, taking these moments into my heart as a treasure to be kept and cherished.

During the Second World War her husband was killed. She became a widow, left alone with the three little girls, one of which was my mother. Sitting close to her and listening to her stories, made me understand the harsh reality she had faced. Yet she lived with such grace and calmness.

She had made a commitment to make a good life for her little girls. Every morning she left early and arrived late from work and watched her girls running towards her when they saw her reaching the little road to home. Arms open wide she greeted her daughters, eyes filled with laughter and joy.

The message was clear to me, "Do what you can with what you have, give unconditional love to your loved ones and live in the present moment". Looking at her, committed to her tasks with a calm, happy and tranquil face was soothing and relaxing to me. I could spend hours there, watching her. The bond between the generations was felt in every cell with a profound, deep understanding and acceptance of the whole person and life as its whole.

Later I realized the power of those moments. The precious moment of meeting, where two humans come together in a level of deep understanding, full acceptance, and joy. I realized that those moments contained such a deep level of compassion, tenacity, and commitment. Through life those moments of meeting have guided me and kept me going.

I have had the privilege of hearing stories of many people, who were able to make their life meaningful - even though the circumstances that they were given, were not optimal.

I have heard many stories of people finding their passion, mission, and vision in life. Starting from scratch, failing, starting all over and finding the power of doing it all again. I believe that life gives us lessons every step of the way.

Albert Einstein said: "I have no special talent. I am only passionately curious". I believe there is a deep wisdom in that quote. Curiosity, willingness to learn, adopt and adjust are attitudes that I believe are important for whatever one does in life. I appreciate the attitude of 'not-knowing', keeping the mindset of growth and accepting life as its whole.

I have always been inspired by the people who are devoted to their tasks, who followed their passion and vision in life. Those who had true inspiration in their souls and mind and had the strength to spread their wings and fly to their own direction and pilot their own airplane.

I have been fascinated by the stories that I have heard from various people, about how they made their living meaningful through obstacles and challenges that life gives and still were able to see hope in the darkness and the positive side of life. Honesty and integrity in words and actions are never left unnoticed. Outer circumstances may vary, but the quality of heart and mind build the bond between us.

I had the privilege to be with my mother at work and listen to stories of various people with different circumstances. As a child, I was fascinated by how people make sense of their lives. Just being present and listening actively to those stories taught me so much patience, broadened my perspective of life and helped me focus.

Traveling through the world and meeting people from different cultures that I really have felt connected with, no matter what their situation, culture or other circumstances were, have brought me back to Mother

Teresa's quote, "Do good anyway. Give the world the best you have, and it may never be enough. Give your best anyway."

Living in the countryside contained many challenges in everyday life. Power cuts, running out of the water in the dwellings regularly and walking to school bus in the dark with wet, cold feet. It taught me how to listen to the signs of nature, how to be consistent and have the grit to go through the rain and the thunder. I learnt how important it is to be of support to each other.

I gained all the skills I have needed in my entrepreneurial journey. I could not have gone to school if the school bus driver would not have committed to taking the cold bus and driving hours on the slippery, narrow roads to bring the children to school. And even before that there was someone who ploughed the streets from the snow early enough to make it possible for the bus to drive on them. From an early age, I saw the interdependence of everyone's work and I learned to respect all the efforts that were made for the common good. Humble and consistent people made their work so that others could make theirs.

Reward was the work itself, the professional integrity, and the commitment to their tasks – the journey itself. Little smiles, a few encouraging words and personal recognition go a long way to show our respect to each other.

The whole system is working and relying on each other's efforts. If trust is broken, the whole chain will break and fall into loose pieces. Every piece or work matters, as in life too. We are here together and not born for only ourselves.

Without someone's effort in other parts of the world, who made my computer, I would not be typing my story with this advantaged technology. I believe that human societies should learn from nature that every piece of the system matters. Inspiration doesn't knock on the door. There are times when we may feel unmotivated, disconnected and our efforts gone to waste.

Doubt is part of the journey, those dark moments of the day when there seems to be no light and no road to follow. Then, slowly, when you feel the presence of the others and you know that being part of the whole brings you comfort, even though you still might be in the dark. Sometimes action itself is the best cure for this, overthinking often doesn't lead us anywhere, action and consistency do.

I started my entrepreneurial journey very early, at ten years of age. I had my tiny business of selling lampreys to the zoo. During the entrepreneurial journey I have had many mentors who have inspired me and guided me with their wisdom, strength, and care.

I have had the privilege of being a mentor to several entrepreneurs and those wanting to become an entrepreneur. Staying humble and still trusting your own voice and mission, is balancing between two poles. Those of being open and still having a solid core inside of you to lean on and the grit to accept failures along the journey. You need willingness to adapt and the ability to keep your core values and actions clean, real, and humble. Having a solid foundation for creating something that is sustainable and meaningful, in business and in life.

Contributing back to society has always been one of my most important values. As a parent I believe we are an example of what we wish to see in our children. Maybe life will throw us some challenges along the way, but children will remember the example their parents have given.

I wanted to encourage my kids to trust in life even though life is not perfect. I wanted them to understand that mistakes are part of the journey, and they are simply learning experiences of life.

Where you put your energy and attention to, there you go. I believe it is important to surround yourself with people, who inspire and support you. And those who also are courageous enough to be honest with you when you are about to choose a wrong direction.

Time is the most valuable of all the assets because we never get it back. So be mindful about how you spend your time, not all activities are serving your cause.

Sometimes it is most important to pause and lay on a couch to let your mind go free and you will find the solutions rather than chasing rainbows.

The journey is rewarding itself, if you enjoy the results only, you miss the joy of the journey. From our children we learn to live fully in the present moment without looking anxiously back or to the future.

Marcus Aurelius, one of my favorite stoic philosophers, said, *"You have power over your mind – not outside events. Realize this and you will find strength."* How we relate to things is what matters the most. Focusing on the things that we can change, instead of giving our time and attention to things that we have no control over, is a decision that is made on a moment-by moment-basis.

Let the past be as it has been, take the lesson and move on, don't let it define what you are or what you can be. Have the courage to let go of the unnecessary burdens from the past and the braveness to help others on the way.

As Seneca said, *"Sometimes even to live is an act of courage"*. We might not know the challenges others face daily. *"And it is in your power to wipe out this judgement now."* - Marcus Aurelius.

Admit that there is a lot you don't know and resist the craving to become an absolutist. Remain a relativist. In life nothing is carved in stone. Never become delusional and try to fight your ghosts, ghosts cannot be fought.

The choice that we make every day is the choice how we relate to things and events in our life. Instead of reacting, we are able to respond to situations that life will bring to us.

Become self-aware. When we know ourselves, we have the ability to reflect on our own thoughts, emotions and values so that they serve us.

Being mindful of our everyday choices we make of how we speak and relate to one another, is giving us a chance to live a fulfilling, purposeful life.

"Nothing in life is to be feared, it is only to be understood. Now is the time to understand more, so that we may fear less." – Marie Curie.

ABOUT THE AUTHOR
TARJA WIKLUND

TARJA WIKLUND is a mother, financier, and entrepreneur with two-decades of international business experience in Europe, the USA, Canada, and Emerging Markets.

She is also co-founder and Managing Director of Finland-based PrivateCap Oy and Director of Myötätuntovalmennus- Compassionate Work Life, also based in Finland.

She speaks Finnish, English, Swedish, German and Dutch and she is learning Italian. She is a licensed psychotherapist, Master of Administrative Sciences and Consult of Applied Compassion from Stanford University and is regularly invited as a guest speaker at international conferences on topics of international business.

Connect with Tarja here:

https://www.linkedin.com/in/tarjawiklund/

PART II

BREAKING BARRIERS AND DEFYING STEREOTYPES

RICHA DAGA

WHEN TECH MEETS ELOQUENCE

As a fledgling so eager

that when she learnt to fly,
no skies were too high.

She soared on undeterred

achieving greater heights,
than what our minds could conceive.

And when she turned around,
to wave back at us,
the pride in our eyes,
gave her wings more power.

*M*y school teacher mentioned the above lines to me as she brimmed with happiness on my selection as a global technical speaker in the Internet of Things (IoT) Slam Conference. She was so proud as I presented among a stellar line-up of CxOs and industry leaders at the IoT Slam'20 Conference organized by the world's largest IoT Community.

Indeed, the primary school girl whom she sent on stage for the first time to give a vote of thanks on Independence Day celebration, had come a long way. She had transcended geographies, journeying from interschool to the national and then, to the international stage. As I thank my teachers for preparing me to illuminate the world, I would like to introduce my life-long supporters and guides – my mother and father.

My father worked for the Government of India's Undertaking, NHPC Ltd. His office had hydro power projects at beautiful places nestled in the lap of nature. I spent my childhood in one such serene and remote place. A pristine valley named Dharchula, on the Indo-Nepal Border, by the bank of River Kali.

I had a panoramic view of the mighty Himalayan peaks. Crossing the bridge on River Kali to reach Nepal from India within five minutes was one of our favourite pastimes. My brother and I used to run behind fireflies and had snakes, scorpions, and jackals living close to our tin huts. It was like living in a forest; we were co-existing with flora and fauna.

My father worked as head of finance at NHPC dam sites and power stations. I was four years old and used to visit the control room, feeling astounded by massive turbines generating electricity with water. This and many other experiences started building my curiosity and passion for tech.

With only one school in that area, we were close to nature but far from basic amenities of life. The school only had a primary level and functioned with the support of the military at Indian borders. When my brother, who was eight years elder to me, reached the age of middle-school, my parents faced an impasse and had to take a difficult step. In order for him to be able to further his education, my brother had to leave us to live alone at my grandparents' house back in Delhi.

Our family saw grief at this separation and my mother had to juggle between living with my father in the hills and my brother in the city. In all this living hither and thither, I was mostly on the move with my mother and was barely able to attend school in my formative years.

My mother used to teach me at home. She was sad that without classroom notes and a defined syllabus, it was difficult to prepare me for the questions in the school exam.

The helplessness on her face gave me an altogether different perspective towards life and education. At a tender age of six years, I decided to prepare and understand the entire school book. Thus, this removed the need to rely on a designated syllabus.

Despite having severely low attendance and competing with classmates who were kids of teachers at school, I topped the exams and the entire class. This brought a smile to my mother's face. Studying meticulously laid the foundation for me to have a great academic career and I started my journey of securing the first rank and academic scholarship in every class at school.

After five long years of work in the hills, my father finally got a transfer back to Delhi. I was eight years old by this time. My father's transfer back and the change of school never affected my academic excellence. I also bagged the first position in my new class. That was even after joining the school in the middle of the year. I felt blessed and happy, owing much to my mother who molded my strong academic foundation. She was my first teacher.

I first discovered my passion for speaking when I went on stage in my primary classes. Debates, elocutions, dramatics, extempore and quizzes were a big part of my school life. This led to winning prizes at the inter-school, zonal, state, and national level competitions. And in many of these events and gatherings, I was recognized as the best orator.

At my middle school level, I brought laurels to my alma mater two times at the state level. I won science fair medals for presenting projects on *Hydrogen Fuel and Magnetic Levitation Train.* You can see that the trend was sustained from the beginning and kept going.

I could understand science and mathematics even four classes higher than me. My parents requested for me to sit board exams under-age. But as a policy of the school, this request was not allowed, and I could not jump classes. I had to continue studying at the pre-set pace. So I extended my knowledge by simultaneously reading a plethora of books.

I took up positions with responsibilities including being the school magazine editor and house captain. I was also selected as the face of the school as its 'Head Girl' in my senior year.

I was a polite girl with an ever-smiling face. I felt glad that the students remained disciplined in front of me as their head girl, not because of my authority but because of the love they had for me.

I excelled in academics, extra-curriculars, and had an all-round performance. I won the greatest award of school for this, which was the Student of the Year award. I was conferred by the leading Newspaper in Education, Times of India.

At the age of seventeen, I cracked most of the coveted entrance exams and had the choice to take admission into the fields of medical, engineering, or research. After due thought and in alignment with the vision I saw for myself, I took admission into the Bachelors in Technology course in Electronics and Communication at a reputable engineering college in Delhi.

Aside from the excellence I pursued, my college life was fun and gave me friends to behold and cherish for life. Even though we are now in different geographies, we still buzz and get along like teenagers whenever we meet up again.

In college, I topped my semester exams and won several competitions in college fests. This was at the state and national level, thus continuing my streak of excelling in academics as well as extracurriculars. My good track record started during my childhood and kept going all this while.

I always believed in giving back to the community and society that helped me evolve each day. Thus, during college, I volunteered in the anti-drugs and anti-ragging campaign; issues which needed immediate attention among the students. I also served as a city guide to foreign delegates and visitors during the Commonwealth Games of 2010 hosted in Delhi. Through this, I received a Commonwealth Games medal of appreciation.

With very few girls in our male dominated engineering college, I worked relentlessly towards a cause close to my heart. My focus was to advocate diversity in the technical field. I became one of the founders of the Institute of Electrical and Electronics Engineers (IEEE) Women in Engineering (WIE) society in my college. I undertook many steps supporting equal representation of women during my role as WIE chairperson.

Whilst advocating for women, I faced a lot of difficulties. It was hard to convince the authorities at my engineering college and the headmasters of various schools to simply send their female students to visit the college. Taking full ownership, I finally succeeded in bringing those girls to the engineering college and showed them the laboratories, the experiments, and the miracles which technology can bring for us. I envisaged that if even one girl takes up science and becomes passionate towards it in her career, I would have done something to contribute towards the future of women in tech.

I organized a national level women's technical paper [presentation for female students in engineering studies. I was strongly focused on my goal to build a female force for the future.

I was recognized for my efforts to bridge the gender gap and was awarded with the Outstanding Volunteer award in Women in Engineering field from

Institute of Electrical and Electronics Engineers (IEEE), the world's largest technical professional organization.

After finishing engineering education, I sought ways to further realize my dream. I saw this dream in the early 1990s when as a child, I witnessed my parents facing tremendous difficulties communicating with my elder brother. We used to walk several kilometers to reach a telephone booth. We would do this in the wee hours of the morning to decrease calling rates. We also wrote postcards that used to get delivered at least seven days later.

Observing this unaffordable cost of time and money, inspired me to do something to help people get connected faster. Technology was advancing and there could be ways to communicate at an affordable cost. I set my intentions and planned to achieve connecting people conveniently at reduced cost levels.

Professionally, I grew up to become a person who is passionate about chipsets and technologies that connect the world. In my decade long experience in Research and Development at world's top telecom firms such as Cisco and Ciena, I contributed to building the internet for the future. I have worked on the development of multiple products that are now supporting 5G, terrestrial and submarine fiber-optic networks. With an ever-growing thirst of knowledge, I also completed my Masters in Engineering in Networks and Networked Systems. I received a special invitation to the convocation, being among the top students of my batch.

I diversified in my corporate career as well. For four consecutive years, I was chosen as the Master of Ceremonies for the annual corporate celebrations that hosted the global leadership of Ciena.

I taught school students from remote areas of India, judged National Level Women Hackathons and organized events to bring awareness for the need of diversity and inclusion in the workplace.

I won different innovation competitions and was acclaimed for selection as a speaker at Ciena's Global Tech Forum. These events occurred internationally. I was very pleased at receiving the Living the Values award at Ciena for exhibiting all the core values of Innovation, Integrity, Customer First, Velocity, and Outstanding people.

In all this determination and excitement, excelling in work and extracurriculars, not everyone was behind me. I had felt pulled back too, not because I was lacking but because I was performing. I realized that giving heed to negative opinions of people can surely make you lose your identity and focus.

Hard to believe, I did leave all my extracurriculars and my so much-loved stage for around a year because I heard someone saying that it is not possible for me to give my best shot at work alongside rocking the stage.

I believed that to excel as an engineer, one should only work around this, and no other personality trait should show up. When I told my mother about it, she laughed and reminded me that I was the girl who won events at the national level whilst securing my first rank in my class each year. She showed me the path to amalgamate all the fields that I love so much with all the characteristic traits that I exhibited from the beginning.

I discovered another side to myself. The will to attain the fulfillment of all the causes that I was passionate about. That led me on to become a mentor, speaker, and author on multiple global platforms and industry forums. Through this journey, I got selected and received recognition as an IoT Thought Leader for delivering multiple talks in IoT Slam conferences on disruptive technologies. I also won the most coveted global conference Speaker of the Year award at the WomenTech Conference held across continents in more than 172 countries. I became one of the core members of SheSpeaksBureau, a non-profit initiative to elevate female speakers globally and address the under-representation of women in the speaker line-up of conferences.

I have achieved much with the passion I have to better the world and serve my tech community. From invitations to author technical articles for enterprise publications to giving interviews on globally acclaimed telecom tech talk shows, I have made it this far with my perseverance.

I derived much of my motivation from the experiences with my parents who guided me to never choose the path where I could lose my identity. My mother, who was academically brilliant, says had she not left her job, because of personal responsibilities, she too could have contributed to society with a remarkable career. I agree, as there are so many bright women who quit their workplaces when other priorities surface.

Today, the world is more aware and comparatively better for women than our parents' times. But it is our responsibility to respect the efforts of our previous generations and not disrespect our education and achievements by being mediocre or ordinary. We owe it to our future generations to manage the difficulties we face, believe in ourselves, and illuminate the world with the spark that we carry within.

Until I come to know you personally and celebrate your story in the making I leave you with the words of Rudyard Kipling, inspiring us to remain inquisitive and become a lifelong learner.

I keep six honest serving-men

(They taught me all I knew);

Their names are What and Why and When

And How and Where and Who.

Acknowledgements

First, I want to thank my family for being my biggest pillars of support.

I am forever indebted to my parents for their love and encouragement throughout my life. Thank you both for giving me the strength to reach for the stars and chase my dreams.

I am grateful to my brother for always guiding me and being there for me. Your support and our fun conversations have meant more to me than you could realize.

I want to thank my teachers at Vishal Bharti Public School, Bharati Vidyapeeth College of Engineering, and Birla Institute of Technology and Science, Pilani for making me the cynosure of their eyes and blessing me to reach the zenith.

My deepest thanks to my close friends for understanding me and giving me memorable experiences replete with laughter.

Thanks to my work organizations and all the colleagues I have had the opportunity to work with, we indeed are superheroes with the ability to bring things to life through code.

Finally, I would like to thank my husband for his never-ending encouragement towards my work and initiatives. Thank you for your unparalleled support while I was chronicling my life story.

I also want to convey my gratitude towards the organizing and publishing team for this book. It has given me the opportunity to pass my legacy through this anthology. I hope to inspire other women to explore their limitless potential and take a step closer towards a gender equal world.

ABOUT THE AUTHOR
RICHA DAGA

RICHA DAGA is an international technical speaker, author, mentor, and engineer by heart. She is a recognized IoT Thought Leader and talks about disruptive technologies at the global Internet of Things Community conferences. She also won the Global Conference Speaker of the Year Award at the WomenTech Conference across continents. She is a technical speaker at the global IEEE Smart Cities Week, ClueCon Conference, and IEEE Women in Engineering International Leadership Conference.

Richa has started and is leading the Country Level, Women in Science and Engineering (WISE) Community of Cisco India, aimed to bring women into leadership roles and improve the pipeline of girls in Science, Technology, Engineering, Mathematics (STEM).

Richa is enthusiastic about technologies and chipsets that connect the world. As a Software Engineer at Cisco, she works in the development of products that pioneer the breakthroughs to build the internet of the future.

Connect with Richa here:

LinkedIn: https://www.linkedin.com/in/richadaga

MAFUNASE NGOSA MALENGA

THE BIRTH OF THE SOUTHERN AFRICAN INSTITUTE OF AVIATION, SCIENCE, AND TOURISM: SAIAST

*T*he inspiration and drive to pursue our dreams stem from a variety of sources. My interest and passion for aviation was deeply rooted in my family.

My grandparents were entrepreneurial. Therefore, they put their mind to creating business ventures and did not rely on a job to fend for their family. They sold tomatoes in the market and did this with so much diligence that the endeavor earned them the income to take their children to school. My father was able to complete secondary education and then proceeded to work at the airport under Immigration (formerly known as the Customs Department).

My family lived near the airport and seeing the workmanship of aircrafts was a norm. Viewing planes as they took off and descended was a regular practice, as I would visit my father's workplace after knocking off from school. During this time, my passion and desire to get involved in the aviation and hospitality industry grew steadily.

Upon finishing my secondary school education, I traveled to Kenya to complete my tertiary education. This was as a result of the fact that the courses I opted to pursue were not offered at any higher learning institution in Zambia at the time. In order to pursue my passion, I had to seek to study outside Zambia.

After graduation there was the need for hands-on training in the industry in order to perfect and hone my skills. Subsequently I secured an internship with Kenya Airways. I was able to do this internship in Zambia, which took twelve months. Then I became formally employed by Kenya Airways and worked there for seven years.

The tertiary learning institution I got training from in Kenya engaged her in a partnership. They employed me to market their educational institution in Zambia. This involved conducting a career symposium at the Mulungushi International Conference Centre in Lusaka, Zambia.

Attendees proposed establishing a higher learning institution that offered training programs in hospitality and aviation within the country. This would reduce the high travel expenses of travel in order to get such education. Hearing these views I proposed the idea to the Kenyan College - to open an institution in Zambia. Subsequently a further partnership was developed between me and the College.

The project emanating from this started immediately with a contractual agreement that also included my husband. All the activities involved in it were completely supervised by me and Shengamo, my husband. In an unfortunate twist of events, the institution failed to meet its end of the bargain and what was intended to be a partnership became a solo journey.

The following year, I employed several individuals to train students in the college; which in the long run was strenuous with regards to the lack of managerial acumen of staff. I had to make the tough decision to quit my formal job and manage the institution full-time; a decision my husband thankfully supported at the time. This decision was made amidst the reality of losing a steady source of income while raising a family.

After countless, tireless, and unending efforts, the learning institution was successfully launched. It was expected that because this institution was the first of its kind to offer training in aviation, there would be overwhelming support from stakeholders in the industry. And it was envisaged that there would be numerous applicants eager to enroll and study at the institution.

To my dismay, none came through and this saw the doors of the institution closed for almost three years. But as luck would have it, the light and hope of the institution were rekindled and brought back to life. Finally in its third year of operations the institution started receiving and welcoming students, which kickstarted the activities of the institution.

Up until now, the Southern African Institute of Aviation, Science, and Tourism (SAIAST) has graduated more than four hundred (400) students. They have been fully trained and their capability and capacity has been tested and trusted. Among these graduates, 80 percent of them are females while the remaining 20 percent, males.

SAIAST takes pride in the quality of its training curriculum and teachings to produce the best products of graduates in the aviation industry. SAIAST has been strategic and productive, with its graduates being employed at the Kenneth Kaunda International Airport as well as at many other reputable and international airlines and travel agencies.

The institution continues to expand as it has been authorized to provide additional training courses. These offer entrepreneurship skills and short IT courses. Both of which are significant means of empowering women; not only of Zambian descent but also beyond the borders. The opportunity to further students' education has also been facilitated by SAIAST's scholarship programs.

The journey appears to be great and accomplished because it attained its final successful outcome. But it involved countless sad, discouraging, daring, stressful, downright horrifying moments and experiences. The truth is, the success we celebrate in people's lives is just a little part of the journey. The true story is a mix of strenuous efforts as well as accomplishments.

In conclusion, although things may not appear easy, it can be achieved. Everything is possible once you set your heart, eyes, and efforts to it. Be prepared to face the challenges and discouraging encounters that will follow. Persevere until you achieve it.

ABOUT THE AUTHOR
MAFUNASE NGOSA MALENGA

MAFUNASE NGOSA MALENGA is the Founder of Southern Africa Institute of Aviation, Science and Technology (SAIAST), CIO Africa 35 most influential women in Tech 2022, Stanbic Bank Women Innovation Award 2022, Woman To Watch finalist 2022 and Country Director Women In Tech Zambia. She is passionate about the aviation industry and has over 18 years of experience in travel, transportation, hotel, hospitality, and airline management.

Connect with Mafunase here:

LinkedIn: http://linkedin.com/in/mafunase-ngosa-malenga-3343b016b

Website: www.saiast.co

ROXANNE CARTER-THOMPSON

TO CHANGE TAKES COURAGE

I will never forget where I was on December 6th, 1989, because it
was the day that 14 women were murdered. They were engineering
students, attending Ecole Polytechnique and they were murdered just
because they were women. I remember the pang of sadness I felt in my
heart for their families and for all women.

Like many other Provinces in Canada, we hold a memorial service in our
community to honor the lives of women who have been lost to violence.
On December 6th every year there is a National Day of Remembrance and
Action on Violence Against Women. A candle is lit for each of the women
who died that day, along with all the women who were murdered in Prince
Edward Island. There is a guest speaker, music, and a room full of typically
the same faces every year.

I went to the service in 2019 like I have for many years. They say ignorance
is bliss, I would have to agree. I knew the guest speaker that year as we had
sat on committees together and traveled in similar work circles.

As I was listening to her speak, it was like she was speaking about
something different. I watched the faces of others in the room, it was
evident that like me, this was information that we were hearing for the first
time. She courageously spoke about her experience of growing up in a
home where she witnessed family violence. I was deeply moved by what
she was sharing. And it was like I was having an out of body experience as I
could almost hear an audible voice speaking to me saying, you're next. I

could feel myself sit straighter in my chair as I spoke inwardly to myself. Oh, I don't think so!

I have already committed my life's work to making positive change. I am not ready to put myself out there and revisit that horrific time in my life. I continued to hear a voice say, it's time. I continued to resist. I said, I am not ready yet. And then I heard, Oh YES you are!

I knew what I had to do. On the way home I spoke out loud the messages that I wanted to share. I have known for 27 years that there would come a time where I would share my story.

For many years, I would drive by a brick building in our community that had a huge painted sign on it. 'STOP the Silence on Violence'. The words on the sign taunted and challenged me to take action!

Through my work I found many ways to take action. I created workshops that empowered women. I ran summer programs that taught girls about healthy relationships and built their self-confidence.

BUT, I still kept SILENT!

I told myself that one day, I would end my silence. I cautiously involved myself in committees where I could take action but not have to be vulnerable. After all, I had a child to raise. And as a single parent, my main duty was to protect my son.

That time in my life was a long and grueling time. It felt like an eternity before I met and then married a wonderful partner who accepted me with the wounds I carried as a survivor.

My son is now a grown man. In 2020 I ended MY SILENCE. I spoke at the December 6th Memorial ceremony.

This is what I shared.

I am a mother, daughter, a friend to many and an accomplished equestrian. I have spent the last 27 years advocating for social change. What you don't know is the cause that led me to the work I do now, it's because I, too, am a SURVIVOR. Why do I believe it is hard for a survivor to speak the truth of their story? I remember the first time I told one of my childhood friends why I left my partner. She looked at me and said, "I can't believe you let that happen to you! You were so confident, you were one of those girls who would never let a boyfriend treat you that way". I remember walking away from that conversation thinking, oh, I'm not doing that again. I didn't like how that felt at all.

In my home, I hid the holes in my walls. I had made excuses for my partner but with my friend, I felt I could be honest. I felt I could be vulnerable. But I was wrong!

A few years later, I was about to date an RCMP officer from New Brunswick. I remember when I told him why I wasn't with my partner. Before I even got the words out, he looked at me and said, "oh please tell me you're not one of those women"? Again I felt that same feeling. And I said to myself, OH, I DEFINITELY WILL NOT DO THAT AGAIN.

SHAME had slapped me in the face.

The messages I was receiving were that this was my fault, I got myself into this situation. I should've seen the signs. My parents fostered, we had children in our home who came from abusive homes. These messages replayed in my mind over and over again:

I should've known better.

I should've prevented this.

I should've seen the signs.

I remember when I went to Anderson House. I was so ashamed to be there. I thought I was telling the individual who was doing the intake a story that she had never heard before. I told them that my situation was different. "The violence didn't happen until I was pregnant. He writes me letters and brings me flowers after he has been violent. He really is sorry!" I found out that day that my story wasn't different, in fact, I was a pretty typical statistic.

I would be lying if I didn't say that it's still hard for me to say the word survivor. Because what comes with that word for me is SHAME.

Twenty-seven years later, I still feel that shame. I still jump when a man raises their voice. I carry a few other wounds, some are physical, some are below the surface.

What Helped Me - What Gave Me Hope?

Twenty-seven years ago, the laws were different than they are now. In 1993, I had to leave the home that I shared with my partner. The law has since changed and now women do not have to leave the family home.

Back then I couldn't put supervised visits in place, because a child witnessing violence wasn't the same as experiencing violence. That law has also been changed. With that said, there is still MUCH more to do.

These and other positive changes have become possible because of the many people who come together every year to remember and honor women. The women who are our sisters, friends, and daughters; whose lives were taken brutally.

I was fortunate enough to be hired to work at 'The Adventure Group'. Working there was one of the best decisions I ever made. It was supposed to only be a six-month contract and little did I know how it was going to change my life. The people I would be introduced to provided me with the opportunity to help many others change their lives.

There were countless people who had an impact on me. I didn't feel alone in my endeavors. People encouraged me to go back to university. They encouraged me to be brave and strong with their words and their actions.

Messages That Supported And Encouraged Me

When I went to hospital with injuries, the nurse said to me "I see you have been in the emergency room a few times in the past several months dear, is there anything you want to tell me?"

There was a friend who sat with me in her car. We were parked just down the road from my driveway. She sat with me until my partner fell asleep so that I could go back into my house. I had to creep back in and say nothing. An innocent comment could escalate a violent outburst from him.

A board member gave me an opportunity to take a six-month contract at a non-profit organization that changed my life. This was at the time I most needed it, twenty-seven years ago.

There was the person who wrote my reference letter so that I could be accepted to Carlton University through UPEI. He wrote that I should be given a seat at the front of the class. He has no idea how those words carried me.

And I am grateful to the businessman who gave me a donation. Later he became a board member and always made time for me. He saw past my insecurities and wounds. He kindly still mentors me to this day.

Shame kept me from telling my immediate family what was happening in my relationship. When they became aware they were very supportive.

The shame that I carried could have prevented me from moving forward in my life if it wasn't for the many people who stepped up and became my mentors, and encouragers.

What can you do to support survivors and help put an end to violence?

December 6th is the day that we REMEMBER but it's also the DAY that we make a COMMITMENT to taking ACTION.

We all have a responsibility to report violence and to support individuals to leave abusive relationships. We can do this by connecting those individuals with the people who can help them.

I encourage you to be the light for someone else. To be their voice of encouragement. To act on that kind gesture that tugs at your heart even though you are tired and feel like you do not have time. MAKE the time. As you do not KNOW how that ONE action or seed that you plant will grow. How it will affect that individual, their children and how it may impact an entire community.

Compassion goes a long way. The people that impacted me the most are not the people that gave me sympathy, it was the ones that provided me with opportunity. They gave me moments to seize, and goals to strive for.

We all have a role to play, I encourage everyone reading my story to think of the role that *you* can play.

Let sorrow fuel you, step up, take the CALL to ACTION and make the changes that are needed. Although there has been progress, there is still MUCH to do!

Note from the author; If you are currently living in a situation of violence, I encourage you to do this. Talk to a trusted friend who can handle the severity of what you are going to share. Along with the support of your friend, call your local Family Violence Prevention Center. Make the call from a phone where your partner will not be able to see the number on your phone. Talk to a counselor or intake worker who can set up an appointment to meet with you to create a safety plan and an exit strategy. Keep   yourself   safe.

ABOUT THE AUTHOR

ROXANNE CARTER-THOMPSON

ROXANNE CARTER–THOMPSON is the Executive Director of The Adventure Group, she has spent the past 30 years working collaboratively to grow a non-profit organization that supports individuals to reach their full potential.

Roxanne was a faculty member of UPEI's Centre for Conflict Resolution Studies for ten years, she has created and taught leadership courses for Holland College Sport and Recreation Students. She also facilitated over 800 workshops in the areas of personal growth and self-awareness.

As a longtime advocate for addressing social change, she was appointed chair of PEI's Poverty Reduction Council in 2018. In April of 2022, she was appointed a member of the Poverty Elimination Council. Roxanne is also an accomplished equestrian who has successfully competed internationally. She has been named Sport PEI's Senior Female Athlete of the year twice.

She resides in PEI with her partner Jeff of 26 years and together they have raised three young adults. Roxanne is someone who believes in living life to the fullest, she wants to seize the moments and truly embrace one of her favorite Maya Angelou quotes; *"Life is not measured by the number of breaths we take, but by the moments that take our breaths away"*.

CATHY DERKSEN

EMBRACE THE COURAGE TO FLY

"How does one become a butterfly? You have to want to fly so much that you are willing to give up being a caterpillar."

– Trina Paulus

The quote of how one becomes a butterfly has hung on my wall for over a decade now. At times when I am feeling down and defeated, I come back to this quote to remind myself that I am on a journey of transformation. It always reminds me that in order to take on a major transformation in life, we need to be committed and willing to leave our realities behind to enable us to move forward into our dreams.

It is true that at times in our life we will question why we have taken on certain challenges. And there will also be times when we want to turn back. But like the caterpillar going into the cocoon, we reach a point from where there is no turning back. Our only option is to move forward in the direction we have chosen.

How many times in your life have you set your mind to taking on a huge challenge? How many times have you made a decision and stepped into action only to be pulled back into your comfort zone? Back into doing the usual things again. How many times have you let the voice inside your head talk you out of following through with your big dreams? How long have you given room for those voices? The ones that tell you, that you are too old, too young, not educated enough, or not good-looking enough to take on your dreams?

On too many occasions, we have let ourselves give in and get defeated. And we have given those inner voices an easy path to win. We have let our dreams and aspirations sit unattended. Left them for another day which does not always come. We have languished more on wishing rather than acting. We have relied more on the endless tomorrow instead of seizing the moment.

But no matter what the situation might have been, I am here to stand with you now to say, "NO MORE!" No more are we going to stand back and let our lives pass by. We will no longer fail to take the next step due to fear or procrastination. Embrace courage! Take action!

For more than ten years now, I have been on my own journey of personal discovery and growth. I follow my heart and my intuition to rediscover who I am and what I have been called to do with my life. This quest has taken me through huge challenges and many paths. It included leaving an abusive marriage, becoming a single parent, making my way through two major career changes, and leaving my corporate job. I have started my own business that is called 'Inspired Tenacity'.

Through these challenging times of my life, I have faced heartbreaks, defeats, failures, and an almost endless state of feeling overwhelmed. I have had to pick myself up over and over again to keep moving forward. I have not allowed my past to drag me backward.

The name of my company, 'Inspired Tenacity', came to me in the midst of those challenges. I realized that inspiration and tenacity are critical components in taking on huge changes in life. We need the inspiration to find our focus and we need the tenacity to just keep going through all of the ups and downs along the way.

The other critical factor required to take on huge challenges is courage. Courage is not the absence of fear but the willingness to take action in spite of the fear. Fear holds us back on so many levels whenever we let it act on us. Our fears can be focused on real issues or they can be focused on ideas that are not based in reality at all. We may suffer from the fear of failure and the fear of success.

Oftentimes, we make up stories in our minds about what other people might be thinking or saying about us and funny enough, our fear is birthed and built upon this. There are so many conscious and unconscious ways that we let fear get in our way.

I made a conscious choice to refocus on courage. It required a committed decision. To be courageous is a decision to act bravely and not give into fear. It required a committed decision.

My life mission came to me when I started out on my journey of personal growth and transformation. It is a goal to create a cycle of wealth and success among women around the world. When this mission first came into my mind, I was not sure how to approach it. At the time, I was working in a medical genetics lab which had been my career for over twenty-five years. It was a big stretch for me to imagine how I would have an impact on women around the world and how I would begin the process.

Initially my intuition led me in the direction of taking on a massive career change to become a financial planner. I had the vision of assisting women in taking control of their financial situation and improving their own quality of life.

In my vision, helping a woman improve her life situation would in turn help her family. By helping families, I would be helping communities that in turn stretched to generation-building and empowering. And as families and communities prospered, they would create a great ripple effect. This would then impact many more people in the world. Thus was born my mission; to create a cycle of wealth and success among women around the world.

Taking on this massive career change at the age of forty-seven requires enormous courage and dedication. With my inspiration and tenacity, I did not fail. In the course of the journey, there were times when I questioned my decision and I felt like resuming the life that I had known. Ultimately, I knew that was futile and concluded that there was no turning back. I knew that I had passed the point of no return; I had burned the boats behind me. The life I had left behind was no longer in existence to return to.

Even in the midst of all my accomplishments, the journey of personal growth and increased clarity evolved. After working for a decade as a financial planner in a corporate job, I came to the realization that I was not reaching the full potential that I had planned. I was not creating the global impact of my mission to create a cycle of wealth and success among women.

Once again, I gathered the inspiration, courage, and tenacity required to take on another career change and life transformation. This led to me leaving my job and this time around, I set out to focus on my business, 'Inspired Tenacity'. It is now the medium through which I am able to help women around the world create wealth and success on their own terms.

In working with women around the world, I now focus on helping each of them discover their own brilliance and strength. And most importantly what inspires them. So many women have lost track of their own goals and dreams simply because they have spent so long focused on helping their families, employers, and communities. This is at the detriment and abandonment of their own growth.

As women we have often been the cornerstone for everyone around us, but have neglected our own vision for the future.

And again, I am here to stand with you to say NO MORE! No more are we standing back to let our lives pass by and let our dreams die! Your life is yours and yours alone. Own it and make it better. Embrace courage, inspiration, and tenacity.

At this time in history, it is critical for women around the world to stand up and speak up. It is critical that we support and encourage each other to embrace courage. It is a time when we must decide what we want, as individuals, and embrace what we are called to accomplish in our lifetime. Don't let the fearful stories or limiting mindsets imposed on us stop us from dreaming big and taking enormous action.

As I charge you to rise up to the task and do what is needed, it is of necessity that I bring you the golden words of Margaret Mead. *"Never doubt that a small group of thoughtful, committed people can change the world. Indeed, it is the only thing that ever has"*. Yes, we can change the world as a group and as a collective.

A quote from Howard Thurman keeps me focused on my overall vision. *"Do not ask what the world needs. Ask what makes you come alive and go do it. Because what the world needs is people who have come alive"*. I urge you to come alive in order to contribute your own brilliance to the world in any way that you can.

Would you say you are living your life doing what makes you come alive? Or have you become numb and stuck in a rut, feeling uninspired and frustrated? No matter where you are currently, let us stand together and say, NO MORE! No more are we living our lives without passion, vision, purpose, or focus. And in this spirit, I charge you to find what makes you come alive and go do it.

Embrace the courage to take on a life that brings you joy. Embrace courage, tenacity, and inspiration now! Bring life to your life! This will create a ripple effect of positive energy reaching out to your community and the world at large. This is our time to shine and our time to contribute to a world that is more peaceful and inclusive. Our time to step into our own brilliance and stand together.

If you are feeling the calling to step into your brilliance, start by building a community around you. Connect with other women reaching for positive change. Make the whole world your very own community to connect with. Supporting each other to embrace courage will create a ripple effect of impact. Stand together and speak your truth.

Again, I bring you the wisdom of Trina Paulus' quote. *"How does one become a butterfly? You have to want to fly so much that you are willing to give up being a caterpillar."*

Embrace the courage to step into your passion. Embrace the courage to fly!

ABOUT THE AUTHOR
CATHY DERKSEN

CATHY DERKSEN is a catalyst and disruptor, supporting women to step into a life that inspires them. As the founder of her company *Inspired Tenacity* Cathy helps women take on the courage to face major changes in their life. Her passion is dedicated to helping women tap into their own brilliance to create lives filled with genuine joy and fulfillment.

After working in finance for over a decade, she left her corporate job and started *Inspired Tenacity* to focus on helping women create success on their own terms.

Cathy is an international speaker and a bestselling author who inspires her audience to dream big and take a leap of faith into reaching for their goals. She has created a platform supporting people to share their own inspiring stories in books, TV and podcasts. With her all-in-one program, Cathy takes you from chapter concept to published bestselling author in a simple, exciting process.

Cathy lives near Vancouver, Canada. She has two children and 2 fur-babies. She enjoys spending time in nature, travelling, meeting new people, and connecting with her community around the world.

Connect with Cathy here:

Website: https://inspiredtenacity.com

Gift: https://inspiredtenacitygifts.now.site/home

LinkedIn: https://www.linkedin.com/in/cathyderkseninspiredtenacity

PART III

SELF-DISCOVERY AND COMING OF AGE

RITA ARAUJO

FINDING TECH I FOUND MY PURPOSE

*B*eing born an artist in times when art is not considered a real job,

except for a few lucky, chosen and influential ones, always made me feel I was not in my place on Earth. I often asked myself if I was really from this planet. I confess that every time my answer was, No, I'm not from this planet. What am I supposed to do here?

Putting my art aside as a hobby, I graduated as a designer, graphic design being the closest field to pure art. I consider graphic design commercial art and whilst it may take the same talent and creativity, the difference is that it is driven by specific goals, not spontaneity.

As an adult, I was satisfied with my job. I could make a living, and always had fun working. But there was this hole in my life, where something was missing.

As a designer my working tools have been computers and software, as well as all kinds of technological resources that change very frequently. Those changes, until now, used to be upgrades of the same tools.

The maximum difference was the transition from traditional media material, to digital. It was during one of those technological upgrades that disruption came into my life. And not just professionally but also personally. My soul finally understood what I came to do in this life and everything transformed. I metamorphosed like a butterfly.

After taking an UX course to upgrade my skills to build mobile apps, I went to my Linkedin profile to update it. A 'crazy' post appeared on Linkedin inviting the audience to get a free NFT (non-fungible token).

I had no idea what NFT was, but a 3D beautiful artistic necklace was shown as being an NFT. Very curious, I followed the steps they were guiding to get my NFT. Then one minute later, the post said there were 100 free NFTs. I was sure I would get one.

What an illusion! The first step to collect my NFT was to open a Wallet. So, I clicked on the one that was shown as popular. This was the beginning and the end of my frustrated journey to have a free NFT. I could not understand the wallet thing, nor what 'mint' was. I had no clue about how to complete the process. It was the most successfully unsuccessful experience of my life.

However, having discovered NFTs, brought me to learn blockchain and the paradigm of web 3.0. It was then that I found FREEDOM.

Since then, studying those new technologies, I discovered a rising culture, a social culture in which the power of the communities and individuals are overcoming the power of centralized organizations. And among all layers of life, the art market is taking a new direction.

For the first time ever, artists had the opportunity to make a living working with their art. Turning their art to non-fungible tokens, building their communities where collaboration is what moves their society. What a fascinating horizon!

At 52 years I finally found my purpose falling into my lap.

The death of my father, when I was 38, had been the trigger of a deep depression that brought me the diagnosis of bipolarity. During those dark days I experienced the feeling of being unable to do anything. I thought I would never recover my capacities, my intelligence or my abilities.

That feeling of being nothing. Most days I couldn't even leave my bed. I have no words to translate the despair of those times. Two facts pulled me out of this hole. The first being my social conditions allowing me to have professional mental health treatment. Secondly, my art.

The medicine gradually got me active again and my art kept me alive by being the only activity that connected my soul and my identity as a human being.

My art literally gave me life. At one time it was the only way I could express my pain and let it flow away from me. My art saved me. All my pain left my mind and became the building block of my artwork. You can feel some of this as you look at the art pieces now.

Experiences of frustration, impatience, lack of focus and concentration, lack of motivation and other symptoms appeared every time I lost balance. Because my routine was often disrupted, my medicine had to be changed from time to time, and some exercises had stopped their effectiveness.

We need discipline and need to make a bigger effort than others to keep harmony in life. And obviously we need support and money. With that we can live a normal life, the same as everybody. I would love to make a living working with my art, but can't quite do that yet. But I am lucky to have support so that I can have a balanced life and keep my sanity.

After doing some research I found out that artists have a huge tendency towards having mental health issues. Or perhaps it's better to say, mental health issues promote a more sensitive perception of the world and life. Sensibility, observation, and reflection are qualities among talent to express this unusual perception. Around 70% of artists I researched have these issues. The majority do not make a living from their talent.

NFTs came to complete the equation of my purpose and were the starting point of my new professional role.

I designed the dxpression business model - a metaverse ecosystem that brings mental health from the metaverse into real life.

The concept came about by thinking about other artists like me. I wanted to create the opportunity for them to make a living and be financially independent working with art. I wanted to build a support community and provide finances for mental health treatments. With these means I could give dignity to artists' lives by helping them have a role in society.

Starting with the name, dxpression comes from depression expression. Dxpression has a mission to teach and support artists with neurodiversity or a mental health issue to get into this new culture and become an NFT artist. To build their communities and to connect them to mental health professionals and treatments, inside the metaverse environments and spaces.

This ecosystem will have a marketplace exclusive for those artists, a gallery and event space to promote the artists. It will be a place to host medical congresses, and all sorts of activities related to the art and mental health ecosystem; a psycho clinic to have sessions and treatments and a pharmacy where the medicine could be cheaper to those artists without middleman costs. A community of stakeholders who will help to make this ecosystem happen. It will support mental health in a new way.

My purpose is to provide artists including myself, our place in the universe inside the metaverse. It will be a new way to experience the internet in the future.

Living my purpose has been a rich journey of knowledge, diving deep into studying this web3 culture. I used to say, the more you learn the less you know. On this journey of love, I've been making amazing friends, sharing with shining souls, and became part of generous communities.

I mix with those who share the same belief that collaboration and generosity lead to a better world. This is a way to change humanity by creating wealthier and healthier realities that share the same goals to overcome those challenges.

'We're All Gonna Make It', (WAGMI), is the name of the dream. Building this new inclusive and diverse society, I became one of thousands of women that are leading a movement to empower each other, inspire each other and become the leaders of the near future world.

As leaders of ourselves, we are conquering influential positions and powerful spaces to bring a more empathic and female way of living into the world. Communities of women like 'All Stars Women', 'Mission Impact', 'MKAI', 'Women in Web3 travel', and so many more networks, who do exchanges, and help and support all their members.

Laughing together, crying together, conquering together, building together the new world that rises ahead. And the most interesting thing about this movement is that it is global, no frontiers limit this network, no culture overlaps others, the diversity and respect is so real. It's beautiful to see and an honor to be part of.

In this new metaverse, no one is ever alone. The new female-governed world is already happening, bringing the world together. Finally, we feel our power, and gradually we use it.

And quoting the title of this anthology, that's how we are changing the world, together we are causing 'The Butterfly Effect'.

ABOUT THE AUTHOR

RITA ARAUJO

RITA HELOISA RABELLO DE ARAUJO is a born artist. Through her life she became a product + graphic + UX + branding + packaging designer and packaging engineer.

She is Founder, Artistic and Creative Director at Oitava Arte web3 and metaverse design and strategy studio.

Starting as an NFT artist in 2021, she became a NFT, Web3, crypto, blockchain, metaverse researcher and advisor. She is also a Mission Impact Changemaker, a member of the team who are Building the USP Metaverse, LOVE.io cryptocurrency Ambassador and Love4youacademy.Ambassador.

As you can see, lots of love in her life. To return all this love and gratitude to the universe she is a Vegetal garden planter and has lots of fun cooking.

Connect with Rita here:

LinkedIn: https://www.linkedin.com/in/rita-helo%C3%ADsa-rabello-de-araujo/

Email: oitavaartedobrasil@gmail.com

VALERIE FOX

BOLDLY GO

*S*cience fiction writers and futurists have always captivated me.

They described a world I wanted to be part of. An imaginary place where technology opened up opportunities, creating experiences that defied reality. Stories wove ways to better understand ourselves and others. They educated and inspired me and I ate up their vision, believing that this kind of world could become real. At least for me.

Fast forward to today and my career is like a testament to that wished for path. I owe most of my career to computer graphics, design and the advances of computer animation. Community learning hubs aided my dreams. As did the special effects that amazed me in the Star Wars films. I was also influenced by Gene Roddenberry's utopian TV series, *'Star Trek Next Generation'*.

I have been involved in the tech space since 1980 where I started as an illustrator and traditional graphic designer. I went back to school in 1983, at the tail end of my twenties to learn computer graphics because of the visionary media influences. I did this because I knew that I was going to be part of a movement that brought the advances of tech and new ways of working to the world of film and technology.

When I graduated, I started a business working with computer scientists and engineers. Our work involved creating user interfaces for training software, using video discs and other now-antiquated graphic media. Back then, computers were only able to portray graphics in black and white, with screen resolutions of 320 x 200 pixels. But over time, the technology advanced and I was able to work in 8 colors, then 16, and finally 256. I remember at the time, I thought that was absolutely awesome.

IBM was a client of mine and after a while, they gave me an offer that I could not refuse – which was to be part of a multi-disciplinary enterprise software design team. I began work using a new methodology called user-centered design. I was on a team that consisted of tech architects, developers, marketing and human factors specialists. All led by a human centered design specialist, Karel Vredenburg.

This opportunity from IBM and the team I worked with changed my approach to innovation design, leadership and working with others. The caliber and diversity of the team members at the time meant that IBM changed how the business and its customers viewed the development of tech.

Technology started to become easier to use, more relatable and created meaningful experiences for the users. It was no longer a mysterious industry that only engineers and computer scientists could understand and work with.

My career at IBM was a lofty one. Although at first, I was a bit of an odd one out. I certainly did not look like an IBMer. I was an artist and designer, uncomfortable in suits, heels, and dresses. Black was my color, not blue and this was not in line with the company's color code. I also had a new, then-unheard-of role in the company called a "User Interface Designer."

IBM employees at the time had two career paths they could choose from, managerial or tech. I chose tech. There was no real job or job description in HR for being a designer. Because of this, I became intrapreneurial – meaning that between assignments, I sought out business opportunities within the company that would benefit by my team's approaches.

I looked for opportunities to advance design thinking and practice into the corporate culture. Ways that would accelerate IBM's software to become more desirable to their customers. By doing this, I caught the attention of a number of champions within IBM. These people supported me in my endeavors and over time I was able to achieve multiple patent awards.

One achievement of particular note was the "Universal Shopping Cart for the Web", which became one of IBM's top 5% patents. I also gained the honor of becoming Creative Director for a host of very large web experiences, my favorite being the Sydney Olympics. Subsequently this led to my obtaining the role as the National Practice Lead for Innovation.

In 2007, Ryerson University (Toronto), hired a new, progressive President – Sheldon Levy. He invited me to jump ship from IBM and come to Ryerson to help in his quest to bring an entrepreneurial and innovative mindset to the university. I knew Sheldon from another time when he was President at Sheridan College and we had kept in touch. This was partly due to our shared love of science fiction and the mindset for extraordinary possibilities.

Sheldon called me into his office one day in 2009. He told me that he had had numerous students and alumni coming to see him with ideas for companies that they had started up. They asked him for mentoring help, space in which to work, and contacts for networking with potential customers and investors. He wanted to help them achieve their goals and asked me to work with him to figure it out. This was the start of the Digital Media Zone Incubator, which was later rebranded "DMZ" in 2013.

We secured a great space in the heart of Toronto. We started by filling it with many student and alumni founders and the teams who had come to Sheldon requesting mentoring. The key founding start-up, Flybits, was led by Hossein Rahnama. He was also a student, doing his PhD with Ryerson University at that time. Many of Hossien's input became the foundation of the DMZ's design. Five other start-ups also joined, along with Enactus, a student-run entrepreneurship organization.

We held workshops and events which attracted more start-ups from outside the university who also joined our growing incubator. Our model was built on having a trusted and welcoming community. We networked with a growing number of incubators locally and nationally. We shared what we were learning and learnt from others too. We worked closely and also reached out to talented developers, financial and marketing experts as well as many others in the entrepreneurial ecosystem in Ontario.

We expanded internationally and brought in entrepreneurs from universities in China, Israel, South Africa, India, and Brazil. Exchanging knowledge and expertise and by doing so, we attracted corporations and governments who observed the latest innovations being developed.

We doubled in size the first year. We tripled in size the second year. And by the third year, we were on five floors with 40,000 sq feet of office space, covering 40,000 square feet. We were helping over 80 companies in their growth and development at that time.

Our reputation soared as well. We were in the media constantly because our start-ups were impacting communities locally, regionally, nationally, and internationally. They were newsworthy because they made a difference.

We created lasting reciprocal partnerships with corporations, organizations, and institutions world-wide. The start-ups benefited from these partnerships and so did the many companies and organizations that worked with us.

I believe the DMZ also helped to create a more inclusive and sharing environment within the university. It influenced the growth of multiple zones or incubators at Ryerson including the Fashion Zone, the Legal Innovation Zone, the Transmedia Zone, the Bio Med Zone, iBoost, and the Social Innovation Zone. These Zones shared resources and knowledge in a way that helped bring multi-disciplinary opportunities to faculties and students. They helped to elevate the university's growing innovative and entrepreneurial reputation at the same time. My work there during this time was an incredible experience.

We were named the number one University Business Incubator in North America. And UBI – a Swedish incubator success measurement company – declared us the third best in the world during our fifth year as an incubator. I left this space after that, in the summer of 2015.

The decision came when I realized that we needed this type of environment everywhere – every town, city, academic institution, and corporation. They all needed to connect somehow; to ensure the success of entrepreneurs everywhere. With this motivation, I started 'The Pivotal Point', which is a consulting company that does just that. We have worked in South Africa, Jordan, the Caribbean, the UK, the United States, and across Canada. Helping to start, foster and grow successful innovation ecosystems that connect to others.

In today's entrepreneurial world, incubators and accelerators bring founders and their teams together into an incredible environment. One that not only brings just-in-time expertise and access to learning, but also access to the collective knowledge and skills of the start-ups. These shared networks accelerated their ability to gain traction and growth.

The new vision and passion for the next stage is as follows.: Once the culture is right, that is, when communication and operational infrastructures are in place, and diversity, equity, and inclusion are in place, and the planets align... then community services, local businesses, academic institutions, national and international corporations, towns and cities can connect in a way that creates mutual benefits for all. Creating benefits that are global, powerful and lasting.

This is the vision of a future I want to experience.

"Boldly   Go".

ABOUT THE AUTHOR
VALERIE FOX

Enabling thriving entrepreneurial communities locally, nationally and internationally through new economic practices of partnership and intentional diversity, Valerie Fox is best known as the co-founder and executor of the DMZ (was The Digital Media Zone), launched in 2010. By 2015 it was named the number one University Business Incubator in North America and number three in the world. She left soon after to found The Pivotal Point where she helps grow community-based incubators worldwide through coaching, mentoring and co-creation.

Val has over 30 years-experience in the digital world, where she started a graphic design business, and then was sought by IBM to be part of their senior innovation network. She led their design enterprise software design teams and was the creative director for large online experiences such as the Sydney Olympics. She was also awarded 5 patents, including the Universal Shopping Cart for the Web.

Other awards include the Sara Kirke Award for Entrepreneurship and Innovation, the 2016 CNE Woman of Distinction Award and the honor of being part of the 2016 Canada Innovation Leaders team.

Connect with Valerie here:

Website: https://www.thepivotalpoint.ca/

LinkedIn: https://www.linkedin.com/in/valeriejfox

SUSANNA RAJ

CONSTRUCTS: MILESTONES MINTED ON MY TERMS

"*Y*ou should come up in life."

A *friend* said that to me. I didn't realize I was down until then.

Another suggested that I was late in catching the bus. Didn't matter where it was going but being too late to catch it was not good, I should do all I can to hurry up.

Metaphors for success.

Their construct for it.

They didn't get to define it. But they didn't worry about that either. It was a construct they accepted and wanted me to accept too. Constructs must be tested and retested according to psychology before they can prove they are valid.

Was this one tested and retested? Did they know more than me? Were they right?

Took me years to learn that they never had answers. Only that I asked more questions than them.

Did everyone six feet under know that they have come up? I wondered.

A lot of that wondering led me here. Writing my anthology for a book. Invited to write as one of twenty women changing the world. I know that I do not meet society's construct of success. I meet my own. I am testing and retesting it to see if it proves valid.

So far it is holding water.

You are reading this. That's proof.

This is not a *'When life gives you lemons, make lemonade'* story. Far from it. This is a *'When life gives you lemons, don't feel tempted to make anything out of it'* story. There is an option to leave the lemons alone. They are not as sour until you juice them. They look lovely as a centerpiece too. Eventually they will rot, decompose, and disappear like all organic things do. Co-exist if you can. If not, ignore.

You have nothing to prove by juicing them and adding sugar. No one to appease by drinking it either; that is the worst crime you can do to yourself.

You have options. More than the ones society lays out for you. This story is about finding them.

If life was all about hitting milestones on time, then I am behind. Missed a couple of them. Skipped a few. Jumped the line for some. I didn't graduate from kindergarten. Or elementary school. Nor middle school or high school.

Did graduate from college though.

Miss. Miss. Skip. Jump.

Technically you must go to these institutions of learning *to graduate from*, and under that condition I graduated only from Santa Clara University.

Fair enough, right? Rules are rules. I followed them—to the extent it made sense.

If you are behind a few milestones, and you have plenty of lemons on hand, and rules that don't make any sense, then I hope this short anthology inspires you.

Here are three lessons I learned from watching and wondering. How it applies to life—and how I think it applies to AI Ethics at the end.

Side Effects

Have you seen the movie *50 First Dates*? If you have, I can skip some medical jargon.

It's about short-term memory loss. Adam Sandler falls in love with a girl, Drew Barrymore. The girl has an accident that resets her memory every twenty-four hours. So, every time they meet again it's a first date for her. It's very hard to impress someone in twenty-four hours, so he keeps failing.

That's my immune system. Every time it meets the same bacteria, it is like the first time. It tries to kill it but, without any ammunition or prior knowledge of meeting this invader, it fails. Then it forgets it failed. Sometimes it forgets to report to headquarters that it failed because of no ammunition. Headquarters thinks the invading party requires a stronger response. They send in the SWAT team and the entire system is wiped out.

Story ends in a few hours. That is how my siblings died.

The medical term for this type of immune memory loss is *CGD, Chronic Granulomatous Disorder*. Google will tell you more but, basically, there are several types of it. One of the best types is the one where you don't know you have it until your forties and sixties. The worst one is what we three siblings were born with; it kicks in the day you are born and gives you a less than thirty percent chance of survival into your teens. Many don't reach age thirteen; my brother and sister didn't.

I did. Not by my own power for sure. Not because of the miracles of science either. That came later. I survived because of my parents' sheer determination to defy the odds. Especially my mother, who literally pickled me inside a sanitizer bottle.

You have seen how impossible it is to hide from a single celled virus, even with a massive, coordinated effort mandated legally on a local and global scale. Imagine doing it without that kind of organized support from society.

Bacteria is everywhere. You can't run or hide from it. No matter what, it found me. So, I spent my lifetime in and out of hospitals.

Mark Twain said schooling *interrupts* education. My education was never interrupted by schooling. Schooling was not an option. Without a legal mandate to social distance, sanitize or wear a mask, school was a suicide mission that I was seldom sent on.

But I read. That's all I did.

Books from libraries, magazines from friends. All wiped in Dettol, the Indian cousin of Purell, by my mom.

And I read the tiny little paper rolled and folded into most medicine packages. Nobody reads those—but I read them. They told me about side effects and adverse side effects, knowledge gained from their Phase I, II or

III results. Randomized trials. Double-blind clinical randomized trials. I knew what they meant long before I knew my nursery rhymes.

Anything that had any printed words, I read. This meant billboards, receipts, epitaphs on headstones. Yes, growing up as a Catholic, cemetery visits are normal. Headstones had very little written on them, but they said a lot. None of the material on their resumes made it there. Only their biological and social relational status was noted. *Loving daughter, sister, wife, mother, grandmother, friend*; the adjective *'loving'* was added regardless of how loving they really were on earth. I thought that was a nice gesture by humanity.

But the tiny, folded paper inside the medicine packages listed death as an adverse side effect. Something to avoid. Only later I learned they failed to mention *expected vs unexpected* as an additional criterion under side effects.

Side effects are normal. Adverse side effects are not normal. One is expected. The other not so much. Life is full of side effects—illnesses, small accidents, nuisances like your home pipes bursting, home fires, broken bones, divorces, layoffs, foreclosures, losing loved ones in old age are all side effects. The adverse side effects are the ones you don't expect.

Twain was right. You can learn a lot without going to school.

Lesson One

Lot of what people lose their mind over, are just side effects. Loss, under most circumstances, is just a side effect. That lemon you can't avoid. It sits with us. We co-exist. You can't juice that sucker and add sugar.

But sometimes it is not normal, it is adverse. It is so sour that sugar doesn't help. Time also does not help. Adverse is defined as *'preventing (your) success or development; harmful; unfavorable'*. In Latin, it means *'to turn against or opposite'*. Something has turned. Not in your favor, but against you. During an adverse event, you turn inward, hold your ground, and try to survive. Survive past it or through it. That is not a time for juicing the lemon, either. *How you survived the unexpected cannot be generalized or modeled for others.*

Lesson Two

What people *see in you* post survival is a clear reflection of who they are and what they are afraid of. Your threshold for the unexpected has just gone up. And the *expected* includes more items now. More than theirs. Many want you to juice up that lemon and prove to themselves (not you)

69

that this is just a little blight, a blimp, a bump, on the road of life. Nothing but a flutter, nothing to fear. That they can rise above it, with no scar tissue seen.

In fact, they are very frightened when you leave it, whole and yellow, on your mantle—and walk away.

Fairy Tales

No one segregated what I read. So, I read a lot of facts and fairy tales. Comics and Encyclopedias. What was common to them both? They all uphold or defy physics. Defy the normal or conform to it.

And fairies always break norms, defy time, to do the impossible for a good cause. Maybe it was the Dettol *or it was* the logic-defying fairies that seeped into my skull—I learned to look past my lemons.

Looking past what is possible is what got me into a number of highly prestigious public research universities in California (UCs) and Santa Clara, San Jose State, and a full ride to another private university.

But Santa Clara won on a technicality.

On our tour, a guide noted the ongoing joke that the garbage liners are changed even before any garbage hits them; that's how clean the campus is. My mom turned to me and said, *"You are going here"*.

Those who don't know the significance of that may see it as vain. But context now helps you see the logic behind it. Context changes the irrational to rational.

In an Asian culture, there are only three paths to their social construct of success. In hierarchical order it goes like this: engineers, doctors and, last but exactly least, lawyers. I chose the *study* of human behavior and thinking, so I can define success on my own.

In my senior year, I chose to declare a second major in art. When I shared this to my cousin, an engineer, he quipped *"On top of one useless major, you decided to declare another one?"*.

He could not see that they are not useless by their own merit, but by the lack of monetary value society will pay for its worth. His construct of success was built on the value *added by* society—and mine was built on the value *added to* society.

Yes, I had two "useless" majors in one degree—and with that I walked into the World Headquarters of Intel to train AI. To answer a desperate call from a perplexed engineering team trying to understand the complex world of human emotions.

There is no such thing as a useless discipline. It is an oxymoron. Check the constructs by which you are asked to live up to.

Lessons for AI

Here is how I apply this to Inclusive Ethical AI:

All learning cannot be generalized. Cultural context is connected to situational context. Everything is not scalable. If speed and scale are your current milestones for innovation, then regulation will etch your epitaph. Humanity will not be so kind as to add the adjective *"responsible"* next to your social standing, whether *you were or not*. Bias mitigation post deployment always appears to me as juicing a sour lemon, adding sugar to it, and asking the public to drink it.

Finally, your repertoire for expected outcomes cannot be shorter than your unexpected outcomes. And we need the tiny, rolled paper inserts for all your use cases. It is about time.

Lesson Three

Constructs of any society are compressed pellets of a time and place, so, I *deconstruct* them. To create new ones that will withstand the test of time and can transcend places. Bringing this knowledge to AI ethics is how I have changed, am *changing,* and hope to fully change its course.

I am not trying to catch any bus. I am neither late nor early. I have arrived.

Up or down depends on where you are looking from. Not my problem. Where I am now, is where I am meant *to be now*.

The lemons are still there. Some fresh. Some disappeared. Fairies don't care about juicing lemons anyway. Neither should you.

ABOUT THE AUTHOR
SUSANNE RAJ

SUSANNA RAJ is the CEO & Founder of AI4Nomads, Women in AI USA Partnerships and Transform Lead, AI Ethics Advisory board member at the Institute for Experiential AI at Northeastern University, and Co-founder & Program Chair of Global South in AI Affinity at NeurIPS. Poster Presenter at NeurIPS 2020 and 2022. She is an independent cognitive science & AI ethics researcher with a background in psychology, studio arts, and human-computer interactions. An inclusive AI instructor at the Business School of AI, a nationally recognized public speaker, and an affective computing researcher with more than seven years of experience. Susanna was a 2022 nominee for the Women in AI North America Responsible AI Leader award and a recipient of the President's Volunteer Service Award 2020. Women in AI Ethics recognized her as one of 20 Rising Stars in AI Ethics and DataEthics4All named her as one of 100 DIET Champions, for her exemplary work in one or more fields of data and diversity, inclusion and impact, ethics and equity, in teams and technology.

Previously, Susanna was a researcher at the Intel Anticipatory Computing Lab and a language data collection researcher at Amazon Lab126. She is a published researcher for the Association of Computing Machinery, the Conference on Neural Information Processing Systems at Women in Machine   Learning.

PART IV

RELATIONSHIPS AND THE COMPLEXITIES OF LOVE, TRAUMA, AND HEALING

DR. NICOLE S. MASON, ESQ.

HEALED TO HEAL OTHERS

"Then your light shall break forth like the morning, Your healing shall spring forth speedily, And your righteousness shall go before you; The glory of the Lord shall be your rear guard."

Isaiah 58:8 – New King James Version

"Nicky, Ms. Georgia is gone." These are words that sank deep down in my heart on the morning of November 2, 2005. My prayer partner was at my door to tell me that my mother had passed away. I could hear myself screaming to the top of my lungs somewhere inside of me, but there wasn't any sound coming out of my mouth. My legs went weak, and I hit the floor. As I lay motionless on the floor, I could hear what was happening around me, but I couldn't speak.

My prayer partner was fearful for me, because I was eight months pregnant at the time. She wanted to make sure that the baby and I were fine, so she called the paramedics. Miraculously, my blood pressure was normal, and the baby was fine. Unfortunately, I couldn't speak to the paramedics. The only thing I could do was shake my head. It felt like my spirit separated from my body. I have come to know that I was in shock at the news of my mother suddenly passing away. Shock is good, because it gives the mind time to accept and embrace a new reality.

As we start our journey together, it is essential for me to begin with the sudden passing of my beloved mother so that you can understand the frame of mind and the heart space I found myself in. My mother passed away from congestive heart failure.

My entire life was built around my mother and grandmother. I was an only child and an only grandchild. Seventeen days after my mother passed away, my grandmother passed away. It was a very devastating time in my life. I am a woman of faith and had been preaching for many years before losing my mother and grandmother. My faith was tested in a way that it had not been tested before ever in my life. The next several years would be filled with ups, downs, twists, and turns that would cause me to dig deep within to find a new normal and a new level of faith.

About three years after losing my mother and grandmother, I went to the doctor for a routine visit. Up to that point in my life, I didn't have any health issues. However, all of that was soon to change. My bloodwork showed a very high increase in my cholesterol, and my blood pressure was extremely high. The doctor immediately sent me to a cardiologist. Ironically, I ended up at the same doctor that treated my mother. Now, I thought I was strong enough to work with him, but that would not be so. Instead of finding another doctor immediately, I made the wrong decision to continue my treatment with them. This would lead to more devastating news for me in the years to come.

As I tried to put the pieces of my life back together, my health did not get any better. At the time, I could not focus on my health. I did not have the emotional bandwidth or capacity to focus on my health and navigate the grieving process simultaneously. It would take a few more years before I could work diligently on my health and make significant progress towards my healing.

In 2015, I felt strong enough to take a deep dive into what I would need to do to focus on accepting my diagnosis of heart disease and doing something about it. I scheduled an appointment with a new doctor. He provided a regimen of medication and a low-fat diet plan. In the beginning, I wasn't consistent with my medication. I would forget to take the medicine. The reality was I rejected the fact that I was under 40 years old and needed to take medication. It just didn't seem right, and I certainly didn't feel it was fair. But, there wasn't anyone for me to present my case to. The only person that I could turn to was God to present my case. I finally decided to be consistent with my medication, eat better, and exercise. My thought was to do it for six months to see what would happen.

While intentionally deciding to take control of my health, I had two encounters that assisted my heart tremendously. The first one was an appointment to see an acupuncturist. My experience was cathartic. During the first treatment, I could literally feel the energy moving in my body. Grief, in my estimation, is a very powerful energy. And, what I have come to know is that so many people get stuck in the process. I didn't realize how deep I was grieving and holding that energy inside me. When the acupuncturist told me that my heart was sad, I cried uncontrollably because I knew she was right. After several weeks, I could feel the difference in my heart and overall in my body.

The second encounter happened during a worship service. A prophet that I had never met came to my church. At the end of the service, he asked for people to come forward that needed healing. I went up to the front of the church for prayer with many others. When he got to me, he touched my hand. I opened my eyes briefly only to see him blowing on my heart! I was overcome with emotion, because I knew that God sent him to pray for me and to encourage me in my healing journey. I had the opportunity to speak with him after the Worship Service. He told me that he could sense that something was blocking my heart. And that he felt the heart-break in the spirit as he blew on my heart. It is important to note that healing is both physical and spiritual.

When I decided to take control of my health, opportunities presented themselves to share my story with others. The first such opportunity was a commercial about heart disease. I shared my story for the commercial at two in the afternoon one day, and at four pm, a representative called me to tell me that the company was interested in my story. After a vetting process, the company flew me to Boston first class. They had a driver waiting for me at the airport, hosted me at a boutique hotel, had a stylist for me, a make-up artist, and scheduled a professional photoshoot.

The commercial took on a life force of its own. It has a few million views online and has been seen in more than 12 media outlets. The pictures from the professional photoshoot were displayed in numerous newspapers, magazines, and on digital billboards located in national airports.

Of course, I didn't have any idea that the commercial would impact the lives of so many. So many people were reaching out to me to tell me that they saw the commercial on TV. This was a way for me to begin the conversation about heart disease with others, especially women of color.

Shortly after that, I served as an Ambassador for the American Heart Association. Working with the American Heart Association has allowed me to speak with the Executive Board of the Association and other top-level executives that support the American Heart Association.

I also participated in a training program to run a five-kilometer race. The training program was chronicled by one of the local news stations so that people could watch the progress. I successfully ran the five kilometers, shaving approximately five minutes off my practice running time. It was an enriching journey.

My story has significantly impacted others. Women have started exercising and making better choices for their health. In addition, I have used social media to encourage and educate women about heart disease and steps they can take to make better heart health decisions.

I have come to know that everything we go through is not just about us. It is about using our lives to serve as encouragement to others. God has strategically placed me in a leadership position to many women. I serve as a leader in my church. I also serve as a leader in my profession. God has allowed me time to work on my healing so that my witness is authentic and impactful.

After being consistent with my medications, exercising regularly, and being mindful of what I eat; I am happy to report that I have lost weight, my cholesterol is stable, and my blood pressure is normal.

I also experienced a miracle at my Cardiologist's office. An x-ray of my heart displayed a cross on it! I believe it was God's way of letting me know that sharing my story with others was my path to my healing. I was subsequently released from my cardiologist's care. I have shared the picture of my heart with thousands of people via social media. I am sharing my story here with one goal in mind: to change lives.

ABOUT THE AUTHOR

DR. NICOLE MASON, ESQ

DR. NICOLE MASON is a fiery and anointed preacher, prolific writer and passionate attorney. She is the author of four books and has been a contributing writer in more than 40 books.

Dr. Nicole is the recipient of the *50 Great Writers You Should Be Reading* Award and has been featured in the *Chicken Soup for the Soul*® Book Series.

Armed with a law degree and an entrepreneurial legacy, Nicole became the Chief Executive Officer (CEO) and President of her own company. Having grown up immersed in her grandmother's drycleaning business, Nicole learned firsthand what it takes to be successful as a business owner. She understands hard work, discipline, and dedication. Nicole operates her business with a spirit of excellence and a mindset to make a difference in her clients' lives.

She has been featured on CNN, Good Morning America, Today, HGTV and Food network.

Connect with Nicole here:

Website: https://www.nicolesmason.com

Instagram: https://www.instagram.com/nicolesmasonesq

Facebook: https://www.facebook.com/nicolesmasonesq

LinkedIn: https://www.linkedin.com/nicolesmasonesquire

Email: nicolesherronmason@gmail.com

STACY-LYN CORLETT

LIVING THROUGH THE LENS OF LOVE AS A POINT OF LIGHT FOR OTHERS

Points of Light

When we have awakened, to God's many points of light,

We baffle at how we could have missed, something so luminous and bright.

Shining like a lighthouse beacon, that guides us safely to the shore,

Aiding us to find our way, when stormy waters steal our oar.

These points of light surround us, taking many shapes and form,

Sometimes as miraculous happenings, that are way outside the norm.

But most often they appear, as a subtle, soft occurrence,

Blending into our daily lives, as small forms of love and reassurance.

Disguised as random conversations, gut wrenched feelings, sights and sounds

All divinely synchronistic, to ensure that they are found.

Little pieces of life's puzzle, that have their destined place,

Transcending time and distance, breaching veils of Cosmic space.

To reach us in the moment, of precise "Divine" timing,

When we most need correction, for our souls' a-ligning.

They provide precise recalibration, through God's quantum light force,

Shining light to guide us back, when we've veered too far off our course.

Igniting the spark of remembrance, bringing us back in the "Know",

Accelerating our forward momentum, with Gods' Grace and ease and flow.

Aligning us once again, with His great plan and LOVE Divine,

Going before, preparing the way, to ensure our own lights shine.

WE are all connected, all made ONE by these points of light,

That serves to illuminate our inner vision, our inner sight.

Our "ONENESS" with God's creation, in unity and love,

All playing out our part, with the Cosmos up above.

So, take heed my friend, to attune yourself, to these most subtle signs,

And you too, will feel the blessings of Love's Lens fully aligned.

By Stacy-Lyn Corlett

*A*s a child we didn't have much in the way of material things, but one thing our house was never short on was love. Things were not easy for my mother and us growing up. Having divorced before my first birthday, she became a single mother of four, leaving her to bear the brunt of the responsibility for raising us and tending to our needs.

Unable to work due to her physical, mental and emotional health issues, she was forced to rely on social assistance and what little monthly amount of money the courts mandated for parental support at that time. Unfortunately, this was rarely enough for my mother to make ends meet, especially with two growing boys in the house to feed. As a result, she often had to swallow her pride and go to the local food bank to tide us over until the end of the month when her cheque came in.

Despite all of this, my mother was still able to open her heart to those around her. Having a soft spot for those in need, she offered whatever she was able to give at that time. She would help lessen their burden, even if it meant adding to her own.

On any given day you would find her taking in stray cats from out of the cold and even stray friends of mine or my siblings, who had suffered some altercation with their parents and needed a little refuge for a few days until things cooled down. All of this, she did without hesitation, not letting her circumstances cloud the vision of her heart to act from a place of unconditional love for those around her. She would take in whoever showed up at her doorstep. Sometimes even giving up her own bed and portion of dinner, ensuring they had a warm place to sleep, and food to nourish their bodies. Her loving, compassionate ways also nourished their souls.

My mother did not do these things for special recognition or her own gain. She did them because love was all that she knew, and it was her gift to give. She did not realize it at the time, but her actions became points of light for all those she helped and for me as well.

Her ability to love beyond her own struggles, demonstrated a higher state of being and interacting with the world around us. Unfortunately, due to compounding health issues over the years, my mother passed away at the age of 57, but she left with us her legacy of truth and a life forged in the light of love. This is where I learned the art of selfless giving and most importantly, the difference that seeing others through the lens of love, could make in their lives, as well as our own.

We learn from those around us in the lives we live so it is no surprise to me that my mother's legacy of love also became mine.

Living through the lens of love not only means that you work to view things through love, but that you also act "from" love. In this way you also affect meaningful change. This love can be in your own life with love for yourself, within your relationships and with others. It can be in your workplace, your local community, or the world at large.

It means working to effect positive change through purposeful actions, that like a drop of water in the ocean, create a ripple effect that expands out in all directions. It can include efforts where actions are taken on a larger scale to effect positive change. It could be organizing a community paint night fundraiser at your local church to raise money for a refugee shelter, or creating a school Talent Show that is centered around fostering personal growth and self-esteem, by working with students where they are at, to help them shine, as opposed to just showcasing the most talented.

It could mean instead of coordinating a short Remembrance Day assembly where staff and students gather together in the gym for a few minutes of silence and the laying of the wreaths, you organize a full, school wide week of Remembrance packed with differentiated learning activities that teach about the importance of this special day and get all classes involved in creating an assembly packed with songs, student dramatic performances, reflective art and poetry, and military guest speakers. Doing this as a way to honour and give thanks for the sacrifices, both past and present, made by great men and women from all over the world, that allow us to enjoy the freedoms that we do today.

Effecting meaningful change in the lives of others doesn't have to be through large scale actions such as those mentioned above. You can make a difference through small, thoughtful, selfless acts of kindness. One such example of this would be offering your friend your complete attention and focus when they need to share their troubles and unburden their hearts with you. Holding space for them to be vulnerable and if needed, being that sounding board through which they can find clarity to help them move forward.

It can be as simple as bringing a sick family member or friend a nice bowl of hot, home-made soup to let them know that you are thinking about them or choosing to forgo your own sleep to get up, change, feed and sing back to sleep your baby granddaughter so that your son, her father and single parent, can get a little extra sleep.

For me it was allowing myself to be a visionary and making things possible by living through the lens of love. When working as the program coordinator for Muskoka Language International Canadian Culture summer Learning Program, I saw that there was a disconnect between the Canadian Staff and Japanese staff. It was like we were all working to do our own little jobs but not coming together as a unified whole to really make the best of the experience for everyone. Therefore, I took initiative to bring forth my own vision for this program.

Instead of having my staff up in their rooms while the Japanese staff and students had their morning prayer and choir practice, I collaborated with the Japanese teachers about having us join them during this time so that we could learn about their culture as well. By instituting this little change, I was able to make the cultural exchange and learning a reciprocal process, making our own learning about Japanese culture and customs just as important as their learning about our Canadian ones.

This small change in priority worked to shift the dynamics of the group. It brought together those working as separate parts to function as one complete, unified team and community. Suddenly staff from both countries were no longer sitting at separate tables in the lunchroom, but joining each other to talk, share and connect both on an educational level and a personal one.

The positive effect of this was rippling into the classroom as well. It meant that the Japanese students were not only engaging more with their Canadian Assistant Buddies, but also coming out of their shell to take risks to use their English language skills. Day by day you could see the entire energy and space of the program shift. By the time of their Farewell Graduation Ceremony we were operating as a unified whole. For the very first time in the history of this program, instead of the Graduation Ceremony just consisting of the Japanese students singing a song in English for us and their Homestay families, we joined with them, to sing a song both in English and Japanese, making the program a celebration of collaboration and connection forged through the universal language of love.

To open one's heart up to the language of love and be in the space of love, so that you can come from love, means being in full connection with yourself at a deep soul level. A connection that opens you up to a space deep inside yourself where you are able to hear the whisperings of a higher power in your life. Whisperings that are sent to direct your soul's own growth and evolution through the lens of love, bringing you into full alignment with the light of who you are, so that you can become all that you were meant to be in this life.

It means coming to a place of understanding and inner knowing, that life is not happening to you, it is happening for you, and through you. To achieve this, you must be willing to let go of the need to control and be in the space of "allowing" all that is here for you, trusting that it is all here to serve your highest good.

Following intuitive nudges and points of light guides us on our journey. When we are able to surrender and be in this place of allowing, that is when the real magic happens because that is when we are able to serve as inspirational points of light and love for others.

During Covid-19, I entered such a space and encountered such an experience for myself. After hearing how our government was offering financial relief to families hit by the mandatory shut down, I couldn't help but feel that our most vulnerable population, the homeless, were being left out of this relief program. As soon as I had that thought, it rippled out into the Universe and the Universe came back to answer me. I started to get little nudging's, the points of light being sent from a Higher Power to guide me towards taking positive action to help the homeless.

These points of light came by way of inspiration from a friend who had organized a Christmas meal program for families in rural areas suffering financial hardship due to Covid-19. This led to a news article that came across my desk about an organization in our city that was working to collect food. The project was to feed those in need through a local church in one of our most impoverished areas of town.

Then I heard a song on the radio with the lyrics, "If not us, who? If not now, when". As these points of light grew in number, the seeds of love began to be sewn, permeating my dreams and meditations with visions. I could see myself standing downtown at our riverfront parking lot handing out sandwiches to feed the homeless.

These points of light were not just coming from me, God was using other people to bring the message home. He was calling me to do something about this situation. I knew this to be true when my daughter's boyfriend told her that he had a dream about me feeding the homeless. When I heard this, it was as if something went "click" in my brain and all of those little points of light came together to illuminate what I was being called to do.

It was in that moment that I surrendered fully to this vision and the "Love Lunch Box" outreach project was born. Everything after that point seemed to just fall into place with grace and ease. Initially I didn't know how I was going to fund this venture. But I found myself winning $560 in the lottery, which was enough to get the ball rolling. So I started the initiative to feed the homeless in my community.

I was suddenly given the urge to reach out to a friend who is very active in community fundraising to show me how to raise donations using social media. Due to Covid-19 restrictions I couldn't use my church's galley to prepare the food. However they did agree to sponsor the event serving as our umbrella of credibility when canvassing local merchants for donation support.

In less than two weeks, my family and I were able to collect donations, purchase supplies, and assemble 500 "Love Lunch Boxes" complete with a homemade deli sandwich, apple, granola bar, juice box and special heart candy treats. The lunch boxes were delivered throughout Valentine's Day weekend to different organizations throughout the city that service this population.

By listening to the calling of our hearts and allowing love to lead the way we did more than just feed the homeless that weekend, we let them know that in the midst of the chaos taking place in the world around them, that they had not been forgotten.

Observation is key. Our eyes are powerful deciders of our world, taking in information and transmitting that information through nerve signals to the brain, helping us to make sense of what we see. When we allow our heart to be our eyes, we are able to perceive far beyond physical sight, allowing us to see with spiritual eyes through the multidimensional lens of love and all of its interconnecting points of light.

A light forged from the pure unconditional love of creation serves to guide us and bring healing to others. Choosing to be a point of light for others by living through the lens of love can affect meaningful and lasting change. It not only leaves its footprint on this earth, but elevates the human condition to a higher vibration. It brings a state of being that works to dissolve the barriers of separation and bring us back to our rightful place of unity and oneness with all.

ABOUT THE AUTHOR
STACY-LYN CORLETT

STACY-LYN CORLETT, is a Multi-dimensional Master of Light Healer and Christ Consciousness Awakening Coach. Using a heart centered approach, she is able to tap into, connect with, and draw forth the high frequency healing energies of Creation and the Divine. Stacy-Lyn believes that the heart is the gateway to healing. It is through the activation of pure unconditional love from the heart that higher dimensions of healing frequencies of light energy can be accessed to help heal the body on an energetic, physical, mental, emotional and spiritual level.

Working within the multidimensional layers of these energy systems, Stacy-Lyn is able to activate all 13 layers, depths and dimensions of her own light body to connect in with these energies, as well as the energy body of her clients. By doing so, she is able to help her clients ignite the spark of their own innate healing abilities and assist them in radiating and emanating more love from within, as they work to raise their vibrational frequency to dissolve negative energy blockages in the body and clear emotional obstacles to freedom.

Connect with Stacy here:

Website: https://www.soulfulwellnesssolutions.com

Email: stacy-lyncorlett@soulfulwellnesssolutions.com

Free download of Merkaba of Love Healing Meditation with Light Language Activation Codes: https://bit.ly/40PMHpD

NAMARA JANE

THE LITTLE ORPHAN GIRL

*W*hen I was young I sadly became a street kid. Growing up in Uganda was tough. My typical Ugandan family of nine children was where I came to understand that there was not enough money to meet our entire needs. Therefore, it was imperative for every one of us to fend for ourselves. We had to do the best we could for ourselves, with no adults to care for us.

At the young age of five years, I moved to live on the streets. As bitter as it was, that was the reality. My siblings also carried on for themselves, tending to their own business as that was all they could manage to do. Luckily for me, after a short time a woman who was my mother's friend picked me from the streets, nurtured, educated, and loved me like her own child.

During my high school life, I tried to find out who exactly I was. This was another tough time for me. I finally discovered that my parents had passed on when I was just three months old. Despite this tragedy, I still learnt to love and embrace life.

I never gave up on my dream of becoming a banker. I kept on chasing my dream and networking with people who were in the field that I admired.

I sat for my high school exams which I passed and thereafter proceeded to the university. This was encouraging as I was progressing towards my dreams. Along this journey, things got difficult and complicated but not once did I give up pressing ahead. Slowly but steadily, I finally graduated with Bachelors Honors in Accounting and Finance.

My longtime dream came to realization amidst challenges and tough times. But upon graduation, I did not get a job immediately. However this didn't disturb me in any way as I believed everything good will surely still come to me. During this time, I would wake up in the morning and get smartly dressed as if I already got the job of a banker. This constant practice earned me the nickname of 'Madam Banker'.

Eventually, after six months from my graduation, I got a job in one of the best banks in Uganda and started working as a teller. At this point of my life, everything appeared to be fine and perfect just as I had wished in all my dreams. My life as a banker automatically confirmed this fact for me.

After working for three months at the bank, I decided to start giving a helping hand to girls on the streets and other orphaned children. I started doing this with part of my salary. I started by buying bread and sanitary pads for them. It was small at the time but I was happy to see myself gradually giving back to the society that gave me a chance to rise and forge ahead in life.

Since I had also spent time on the streets, I easily connected with the children and understood what they went through. I could still vividly remember the story of how the girls got raped on the streets, how they were constantly beaten by the drunks, how they were constantly exposed to the horrors of the night. Their stories motivated me to always give my best to help them in any way that I could.

I worked tirelessly to help these people and I devised several means through which I could give them that total and relieving support. It was with this passion and quest that the "Hands of Hope" was birthed in the year 2018.

I founded the Hands of Hope with the African proverb in mind that says, "the wind never forgets the source of the water", which means never forget where you came from.

For me, Hands of Hope was birthed as a way of giving back hope to those that had lost hope, those who think that being an orphan or a street child is the end. While helping them, I also tirelessly helped them to believe that all hope is not lost from their lives. When I held onto hope and saw it come through for me, then their own hope of a better life was bound to be a sure thing. I believed in them, until they could believe in themselves.

After one year working with the orphaned girls and street children through the foundation of Hands of Hope, I sadly learnt the fate of my late mother. She was given out for marriage at the early age of fifteen without having a chance of going to school. As devastating as this news was to me, it also motivated me to take further actions. Motivated by this, I went on an investigation and found out that this barbaric practice still went on in my home village. I discovered that many innocent girls like my mother were victims of this sad reality and helpless to do anything about it. Hands of Hope added the responsibility of fighting for these helpless and suppressed persons in order to liberate them and put an end to this bad practice of child marriages.

Hands of Hope is an all-inclusive charity, fully focused on liberating and empowering women through all possible ways. Hence, we are consciously assisting in building, raising, and nurturing a community of resilient, self-reliant, independent, successful, and educated women and girls. In this light, we work with marginalized and vulnerable girls and women in and out of school.

Since the inception of Hands of Hope, we have positively impacted over 15,000 lives. We have helped with education and skills on income generation, farming, financial literacy, menstrual hygiene management, sexual reproductive health and gender-based violence. We have also supported many girls with scholastic materials and sanitary pads both in schools and rural communities.

Hands of Hope has also come to the rescue of girls and women in the rural areas of Uganda that use old mattresses, banana leaves and tissues during their menstrual periods. In our menstrual health crusade in these areas, our slogan is "You can send women to the Moon and Mars later. But first provide sanitary pads for them."

Through Hands of Hope, we have also empowered women beyond just their basic needs. We have gone further to empower them in terms of agriculture through which nutrition and food security is guaranteed in their rural areas. Women have also been empowered in areas such as investment, expansion, and in other areas of women empowerment and sustainability. All thanks to the many amazing friends, partners, and collaborators that have brought these achievements come into being.

From being an orphan, I have journeyed through life and made the most of it; helped and empowered others in limitless and unimagined ways. My message to all girls and women across the globe is - never give up. Keep chasing your dreams, believe in yourself, do whatever it takes and network with people. Keep optimistic and know that one day, the sun will shine bright on you and bring that your very own, especially being into a fulfilled existence.

In conclusion I would like to say to you that if a homeless orphan could rise to prominence and empower over 15,000 lives and keep doing more, you too can do more. You can do this no matter the state of things with you.

Thus, I challenge you to rise up and conquer and go out and impact the world positively. What is your dream for yourself and others? Find this purpose and go forth and make a difference in the world.

ABOUT THE AUTHOR
NAMARA JANE

NAMARA JANE is a born-again Christian who has now spent five years serving God and the community by empowering vulnerable and marginalized women, children and adolescent girls. Jane has encountered many challenges right from living with her family on the streets to now working with different marginalized communities. This hasn't ruined her dream and passion.

Jane is the founder of Hands of Hope. She has a Bachelor's degree in Accounting and Finance from Makerere University Business schools and is an auditor, tax consultant, and certified accountant with the Uganda Institute of Certified Accountants.

Jane has realized her call and passion of serving marginalized women and girls, who live on the streets she came from, as a means of inspiring and empowering them. Today she is sharing her journey with the hope that it will inspire other orphans and street children to work towards their dreams.

Connect with Namara here:

Website: https://hoha.org.ug

Linkedin: https://www.linkedin.com/in/namara-j-849519120/

DAKSHIMA HAPUTHANTHRI

RAINBOW IMMIGRANT

*S*ri Lanka. That is the island I was born on. As the first and eldest child, I was the first treasure among all treasures to my parents. And as some parents do, when I was born, my grandfather checked my horoscope from an elder in my mother's village. He was told that "this child would go far in the world and will make her mark".

While I was growing up, nobody asked or told me to be perfect but I knew I had to be. I wanted to be the best sister for my only sister and the best daughter to my parents. I knew this would help build a great foundation leading towards a great life with both family and society-wise.

Having short hair and being tomboyish in nature, I liked to play cricket with boys. I did things that were normally expected from boys. And to this day my grandmother still reminds me how I hid behind walls with black ashes all over me, while playing out and hiding away from her. These were early signs of becoming the cheeky black sheep of the family.

As a child, aside from my playing, explorations and adventures, I liked to study, read, and learn. My childhood was blissful and for this I am thankful to my lovely parents and extended family who showered me with endless love, care and tenderness.

I was given the right teachings and upbringing. My childhood was great in so many ways. During my early teens, my parents sent me to an all-girls school in Colombo; the commercial capital of Sri Lanka. This period of transition helped me realize so many things about myself. It was also during this period that I first discovered I was queer.

I was in love with a girl which is a forbidden thing in my country of birth. And for this love that I held, I was mocked, bullied, and rebuked by others. They saw me as being abnormally different.

I was shunned and my love was lost. This was when I first started self-harming; cutting my hands with razor blades and wrapping them up in bandages. I was already hated, ignored, and left to my own world. And so nobody knew about this nor asked why I was sad. All these acts even escaped the loving eyes and usual attention of my dear mother.

At sixteen, at the British Council Library, I read a book, 'Funny Boy' by a Sri Lankan Canadian author called Shyam Selvadurai. In the book, he told a story of a same-sex relationship and this was the first time in my life I had read something like that. It was eye-opening and over time it helped me to figure my life out.

After high school, I was opportune to be among those selected to go to the university to enroll in a Bachelor of Arts. Subsequently, after completing a very competitive examination I was also selected to go to a highly prestigious law college. I chose and focused on the study of law which defined and changed my life from thereon.

During the Criminal Law Class, I learned about the Sri Lankan Penal Code which was prepared and given to the Sri Lankans by the British colonials in 1883. According to section 365A, the Penal Code prohibited homosexuality. An activity which I had almost engaged in earlier on. Homosexuality according to this section is an offense that is punishable by rigorous imprisonment.

Alongside the rigorous process and expectations in the law college, I faced many emotional heartaches and challenges. My relationships during this time were never successful and always ended up in hurt and heartbreak. These emotional complications piled up on me until I could not take it anymore. I decided to end my life during the first-year finals of my law college. I took an excessive overdose of painkillers to hasten up the process of taking my life. Excruciating pains followed but in all I survived it. And with a heavy heart I still had to live. I had to endure the life that I had wanted to run away from.

My life was beyond my comprehension and I felt I could not handle it. I could not share how I felt with anyone as I feared judgment and ridicule. Therefore, I hid these things and took solace in my self-made closet. Constantly lonely and sad, I felt surviving alone was not meant for me at all. But I carried on.

My parents suggested the idea of marriage. Aside from me benefitting from it, they would also benefit because it meant that I would start a family and they could become grandparents. That was their dream. I was fortunate enough that they did not push me or this dream too hard. And for that, I am thankful to this day.

Gradually, this challenging time of my life rolled away. I later joined the bar thereby making my parents proud. With no further delay I started a legal practice in my hometown. I gave voice and hope to the voiceless, poor and helpless. By taking on many pro bono cases, I helped the oppressed, suppressed, and those longing for liberation.

At the peak of my buoyant career, I met another lawyer whom I fell in love with, someone who was already married. As love is blind to all things, I proceeded with the relationship. Later, I realized that I was living a lie.

I lived that lie for almost seven years and many times contemplated marrying a man and living a double life. This occurred to me as a way out to be with the person I loved. Perhaps it was a way to live with a sane state of mind and get on with life in a way that could proceed well and smoothly.

For me, love is worth all the sacrifices I can make. But while love is supposed to be celebrated, I was only but a mere footnote in someone else's life story. Unfortunately, I went along with everything.

To break this vicious cycle, the person I loved then, suggested we migrate. The plan was for me to go first, and then, they would follow suit alongside their family. I was very excited about the whole development and immediately planned my departure and escape so to speak.

Acting on the plan, I tried to migrate to Australia which did not work out. So later I chose to migrate to Canada. It was a random choice made in the midst of wanting to actualize my migrating plans with my lover.

With the pursuit of going to Canada coming to fruition, I just jumped into a plane and flew down there. I left everything behind including my loving parents, only sister, my legal career, and the person I loved the most. All with the hope of everything working out.

I thought, this is it, my new and exciting life. My plan was to start practicing law immediately after I landed in my new location. Fate, as always, had other plans for me. My dreams were short-lived. I could not practice the law as Canada demanded me to start law school from afresh and sadly, I did not have the money or the time to start everything from scratch.

I was losing my mind when I left the Faculty of Law, University of Calgary until I saw the name 'Faculty of Social Work'. I went in and met a student advisor who through our conversation told me about the University Transfer scheme. With it I could start school in Canada from the third year. Immediately, social work seemed like the right calling for me and it became another defining and significant decision.

In the Spring of 2017, I started my fourth degree. I was going through so many changes. My social status was gone. There were big time differences from back home. The weather was the total opposite, instead of being hot I experienced my first freezing winter. I undertook survival jobs and had a very hectic schedule.

All of these factors affected my long-distance relationship. Instead of a loving one it was filled with mistrust, gaslighting, harsh and cruel words, fights and slamming phones. I cried, I felt miserable. But I allowed endless and increasing abuse. Sadly, I was getting used to all this while my life was a mess. I was all alone and my mental health was deteriorating.

Then, I did something I am thankful for up till this day. I started watching "Orange is the New Black." For those who do not know, it was a prison drama on Netflix by Jenji Cohen. It lifted my spirits. There was a huge fandom on Instagram for the show. Fans were rooting for Laura Prepon who played the character of Alex Vause to start a relationship with Taylor Schilling who played Piper Chapman.

One tragic day, Laura Prepon announced her engagement to a man; an actor named Ben Foster. I was among millions of broken hearts who watched the show. I posted on my Instagram that any of the fans who wanted to talk about this tragedy should connect with me. One person from the UK reached out among others.

As months passed by, my new and good friend from the UK noticed something in me. My bubbly and fun-loving personality was gone. She prompted me to go see my family doctor and I was diagnosed with mild depression. Medication was prescribed immediately for me as the next step of the process.

After a few months, I began to realize that I was stuck in a highly toxic, abusive, and exploitative relationship. It was within this moment of deep reflection and realization that I concluded and decided to end my long-distance relationship which was the primary source of my depression.

After this difficult but defining decision I was able to start a healthy relationship with no other person than my good friend who is in the UK. We both had selfless and unrequited love suppressed in our hearts. We have been together now for four years.

With this going on, I decided to open up to my parents now. Both of them reacted differently. As for my mother, she cried for months. But wanting the best for me, she gradually started to support my partner and me. As for my father, he refused to discuss it further.

As a person who thought there was something wrong with me because all my relationships ended on a tragic note, I thought it was not possible for me to love someone and call them my own. Being in Canada truly helped me embrace who I was. I am a cisgender lesbian and proud to be able to say that out loud without looking over my shoulder with fear. Today, I live a life full of contentment with the person I love. My dreams have come true in full realization.

I am a social worker now and I have created my own support system for folks who are coming out through www.dilipani.com medium. Dilipani is my middle name which means "the lighted lamp." As a person who was scrambling for a little flickering light to guide my way, I know how hard it is to lose hope. Especially when you come out to your loved ones and don't get the support you need without judgment. I am guiding and supporting those who need to find their voice. I want that for my younger self but could not have it, for I lacked support from those around me. Hence, I decided to give out my total support to those walking or who had walked my path.

Aside from my story and experience-induced focus in life, I am also a motivational speaker and support many nonprofits and other organizations to normalize vulnerability. I do this by sharing my life journey and having honest conversations about mental health which is taboo in many cultures.

I am a huge fan of the Japanese art form "kintsugi" where broken pottery is mended with gold. As individuals, we all go through tumultuous journeys, but our struggles make us who we are. They make us stronger and more resilient. And as women, we are indeed changing the world. By not rushing to the finish line on our own, we can support one another and better represent our mothers, grandmothers, and future generations.

My younger self would be extremely proud of me today. Never thought I would be able to speak out loud to the whole world about how tumultuous my journey had been, but here I am.

My father finally started talking to my partner, not with too much enthusiasm but we will get there. Still standing tall and proud and not giving up, I am being my authentic self. I am blessed. Thus, I will say that with hope and persistence, anything is possible!!!

ABOUT THE AUTHOR
DAKSHIMA HAPUTHANTHRI

DAKSHIMA DILIPANI HAPUTHANTHRI is a former lawyer from Sri Lanka. Now, she is a registered social worker and a social Justice advocate who lives in Calgary, Alberta.

She has created "Dilipani", a supporting network to provide guidance to those who are struggling to come out with their sexual orientation and identity. She helps to bridge the gap between them and their families. As a person who has gone through tumultuous challenges and trauma of coming out herself, she wants to create safer space and be the guiding light to anyone who needs her support.

She is also a guest lecturer, motivational speaker, and facilitator who has worked closely with many non-profits and Universities in Calgary.

She lives by the motto "We rise by lifting others"

Connect with Dakshima here:

Website: www.dilipani.com

Linktree: linktr.ee/Dilipani

PART V

MOTHERHOOD AND WORK-
LIFE BALANCE

JANIS F. KEARNEY

MISS ETHEL'S HARD RULES: AN EXCERPT FROM LIFE

*A*not so funny thing happened in 1969, during my mad dash to become a grownup. It was something that horrified me, and gratified me. Most importantly it taught me that mothers are neither the monsters, nor the invincible superheroes we so often make them out to be. Later, when I became a mother myself that became the best source of demystifying motherhood.

It was 1969, that taught me such important lessons about my mother. It gave me a new perspective and, no matter what happened after that year, I never saw mama, or her life-controlling household rules in the same way.

Ah, Ethel Kearney's omnipotent rules. Whether it was mama's household rules, my own adolescent hormones, or my anxiety to be a grown up; for years, the two of us would co-exist in a silent, but caustic tug of war. I would continuously tell myself that my hate for mama's rules nullified my love for her.

Had I dared to list Mama's endless rules during that time; those lined white pages of my school notebook would have stretched from the farthest wall of our family outhouse to the front wall of our living room. A distance of about 300 yards. The living room was where our 12-inch black and white television sat, and where the Kearney children spent Sunday evenings watching Marlin Perkins's '*Wild Kingdom*'. During weeknights my father mesmerized us with his own amazing tales, before we were shooed off to do homework.

Mama practiced the "One Lesson- One Rule" kind of parenting. She only told you once, but fully expected that one lesson to stick forever. Or, at least until you no longer lived in the Kearney household. If she ever had to tell you any one thing a second time... just take my word for it, you did not want to be a slow learner in the Kearney household.

The craw that stuck in my throat, was not simply that Mama's rules were archaic. Cleopatra's mother surely delivered those same edicts to her child some 2,000 years ago. It was the blatant inequity in the way she parceled out her gender-based rules to her 11 boys and eight girls.

While I was nowhere near as brilliant as others in my family I could easily see the brazen gender inequality in Mama's arc of justice. A flower child at heart, whose mantra was "fairness or die"; I seethed at mama's injustice. Her rules, favoring her boys, brought out the innate feminism in me – even before I knew there was such a word. For my brothers, it seemed to me; there were virtually no rules about dating or staying out late on weekends; or spending the night with friends at a young age. In stark comparison, my first date was months after I graduated from high school.

There was a boyfriend, of sorts, during my high school years. But, that dating period was so constrained I wasn't a bit surprised that I never heard from him again after graduation. The look my parents gave the poor boy as he walked through our front door on those Sunday nights couldn't be construed as anything other than hostile.

They may as well have blurted it out - you are being watched. The rules were crystal clear. A two-hour visitation pass would be voided when the 10 o'clock news came on. By the time the broadcaster was reporting his first story I was at the window, watching my boyfriend's tail light as he drove out of the front yard.

To their credit, my parents had relaxed their usual rules of NO BOYS allowed in their home after dark. And, I can imagine they were quite flustered by the boy's gall, as he was bold enough to arrive at their home like clockwork on Sunday nights.

While I wasn't exactly clear what the word 'feminist' actually meant back then, I knew it had something to do with brave women railing against how women were short-changed in life simply because they were women... or, girls. Admittedly no one who knew me thought I even remotely reminded them of a young Shirley Chisholm, or Fannie Lou Hammer; and certainly not Angela Davis - given the fact that my parents refused to let us girls style our hair into that beautiful, perfectly rounded, Afro style that helped pivot

Angela onto the international cultural stage. Nevertheless, if I could have, without fear of retribution, I would have expressed my deep sense of injustice.

But, because I was not a brave feminist, and because my mother didn't believe in sparing the rod - I became a genius at thinking hard, and saying little. And, sometimes of using my silence as a form of manipulation, a young manipulative feminist. Forty years later, I can admit that the 16-year old me was a two-faced, cowardly child. What you saw on the outside, wasn't necessarily expressive of what was going on inside.

Never, ever would I have openly protested my mother's rules. I am still remembered by neighbors as 'one of Miss Ethel's good girls, who never gave her much trouble.' My neighbors were clever at observing my behavior, but not much good when it came to reading minds.

I *was* good, in fact... methodically following Mama's rules as long as she was within listening or watching distance. But, once I was out of her sight and sound, I let my rage soar. I used every curse word I'd ever heard, savoring the feel of those nasty, ugly words in my mouth. Only quiet contempt teaches us how to roll our eyes so dramatically that our parents threaten to knock them out of our faces.

One of my proudest forms of protest was going sometimes days without speaking one syllable to a living soul. Not that I wouldn't follow every one of mama's directives on those days... I just wouldn't affirm to her that I was doing it.

To be honest, my 24-hours of silence didn't phase Mama one bit. I mean, she had a passel of children who talked and argued and fought inside and outside the house from morning till night. One 15-year old girl who actually kept her mouth shut 90% of the time? Well, she hardly noticed. Such a protest flew right over Mama's pragmatic, no-nonsense head. Subtlety works in some households, but not in homes with ten or more children with loud mouths, diverse and strong opinions. And parents who wield with iron fists.

Funny, how fifteen doesn't last forever. One day, in the midst of this one-sided tug of war with my mother, everything – or, it seemed like everything at the time, suddenly changed. I woke up a child that morning, but by night, I was virtually a grownup with knowledge that only an adult should ever have to grapple with. Suddenly, Mama was far more important than her rules and was far less invincible. I realized that mama wouldn't live forever. More importantly, I would realize that her life had never really revolved around confounding our lives with her rules.

I had been the blind and self-absorbed one. Defining Ethel Kearney by her mastery at rulemaking and dispensation and defining myself by my level of manipulative acumen. I will always remember that day by how, in sheer cartoon-style, the oversized word floated above me: C-A-N-C-E-R. There is no doubt that I'd heard the word before, but it had not been one I would have held onto. I liked beautiful words— recalcitrant, cello, molecule, perpendicular— those I had pocketed over the years and never forgotten.

It wasn't until that Fall day, when I learned how small and human Mama was, that I finally embraced the word like a strange and unwanted member of the family. It was then that I took a long, hard look at this uninvited word. As I did with most words, I rolled it around on my tongue first; inspected its weight and smoothness, before absorbing and accepting its worth.

It was 1969. No one had introduced this strange intruder into my world. No one had joked about how unattractive it sounded. Not the comedian on Ed Sullivan's show. Not my high school teachers, and certainly not our minister at Rankin Chapel Church.

Fifteen-year-olds are notorious for lying to themselves about how smart and grown-up they are. Back then, if anyone dared question my maturity or intelligence, I'd fix them with one of those Betty Davis or Greta Garbo stares I'd swiped from some evening matinee. The look that says, you're obviously too blind or too much of a fool to see how amazingly smart and sophisticated I am.

It was one thing, imagining at fifteen that I was far smarter and more of an adult than I really was. But there was something else. I was ashamed of how much I loved and admired my mother. Something I would never, in a million years, have admitted. In my eyes, Ethel Kearney was not just bigger than the world, she was the world. The Clint Eastwood of the Kearney household - a woman who rarely spoke, and when she did, never in a loud voice. Stoic is how many described this small, pretty woman who demanded respect and awe from not just my father, but from her whole brood of children and the community around her.

In spite of how much others held Ethel Kearney in awe; I refused to reveal my own feelings, hiding them deep inside. And because I was naturally a quiet child, it wasn't so hard to do. Not even my best friend, Linda, who was the first to learn I had kissed a boy. Nor my sister, Jo Ann, who was my best friend until our teenage years when she became my arch enemy. Certainly not my brothers, who watched Jo Ann and me like hawks. And with glee, squealed our large and small sins to Mama.

No. Not a soul suspected that I worshiped the ground my mother walked on. And, there was absolutely nothing you could do, short of threatening me with a slow and horrible death; or gouging my eyes out, (ensuring that I'd never read another book), to force me into admitting such a thing.

But, then came the CANCER. I wanted to but could find no palatable way to ask other girls in my class whether they had encountered this horrible intruder in their own homes. Somehow, I didn't believe they had. Instead, I was convinced that this was a personal thing between God and me that he'd singled me out as a sinner. Surreptitiously striking the one most important person in my life; all because of my cowardly lies and pretenses over the years.

I knew the cancer didn't affect me in the same way it did Mama, yet, it changed me in significant ways. I knew what I had to do - seek a truce with my mother and try for an honest relationship. Maybe, if I was lucky enough, forge a kind of friendship, if such a thing was possible. Most importantly, I knew it was a warning that I must atone for my cowardly sins.

I did. God actually listened to my pitiful prayers, my apologies and promises late at night. I prayed alone when I knew Jo Ann, Jeff and J.D. who shared my bedroom, slept. I had God's ear all to myself. It was only during this time –those hours between a child's sleep, and morning— that I dared open up about my fears.

I shared my fears for myself, and for mama. It was then that I allowed myself to remember with fresh pain how hurtful my quiet hate had been, even if mama never knew it existed. As my younger siblings slept and dreamed of tomorrow, I prayed for a way to change yesterday. A 15-year-old pretender, wrapped in old sins, bargaining with God for redemption and grace.

And yes, He heard me. The sacrifice, however, was my mother's left breast which was removed. That breast had been sustenance to all of her 18 children. From the son she bore at the age of 17, to her last child, Judy, born two months before her 47th birthday. Daddy never told us what that loss meant to him, but I imagined it was different from her children's loss.

Without understanding why, I had been spared so much. My atonement was a rite of passage; one that hurried and authenticated my maturity.

I served as my mother's caretaker through her next months of healing. Spending the morning hour before I caught the yellow bus to school, changing the dressing on mama's now-flattened wound. We switched roles for a time. I became the mother and she, the dependent child. And, nothing in this world could have made me understand her value, her worth, more than that odd reversal.

Cancer, or God – or, maybe some strange collaboration between the two, forced my fifteen-year-old self to push aside my childish grief. Setting aside myself and caring for Mama allowed me to grow up - not merely pretend I was grown. I was no Joan of Arc, or Sarah Bernhardt, or Mother Clara or Sister Teresa… I was just a child learning how to be a woman, paying homage to one woman who mattered more than life itself.

It was during that horrible but amazing experience that I learned what she had tried so hard to teach. I was able to see something in us both that I'd been too blind to see. My need for a mother and her need for her child showed that we were more alike than I ever could ever have imagined.

Those next ten years were truly magical, as we forged that friendship I had prayed for and had needed so desperately. She and God forgave me for remaining a young fifteen for far too long, and for remaining blind to Mama's simple lessons.

On the night that we said goodbye, days before the rest of her family and friends, I sat beside her bed. Her face, flush with love and resolution. Mine with tears standing but refusing to fall. Her beautiful face, unbelievably youthful, was crowned by short, silvery curls. She touched my hand, looked into my eyes. "Remember… remember everything," she said.

The rules, the lessons? I wasn't certain but was certain it didn't matter. As we smiled across the hospital bed, it was as if we stared into each other's mirrors. "I'll remember, Mama,"… that the lessons, and sometimes the rules, are the most valuable gifts that mothers can offer. I will always remember, Mama.

ABOUT THE AUTHOR
JANIS F. KEARNEY

JANIS F. KEARNEY, writer, publisher, writing instructor, and literacy advocate, is a native of a rural Arkansas town. She grew up in an extremely poor household and graduated from Gould Public Schools, and the University of Arkansas at Fayetteville with a B.A. in Journalism.

She served nine years as a project manager and public affairs director for the Arkansas State Government. She later served as managing editor for civil rights legend Daisy L. Gatson Bates' historic *Arkansas State Press Newspaper*, then as publisher and owner of the newspaper.

Janis worked eight years in the William J. Clinton Presidential Administration. She served as director of communications for the US Small Business Administration, then, as President Clinton's personal diarist—the first-ever personal diarist to a president.

In 2001, Janis was selected as a fellow at the W.E.B. DuBois Institute of African and African American Studies at Harvard University. She is a founding member of the Little Rock National Association of University Women, a native of Gould, Arkansas.

She and her husband founded Writing our World Publishing, a small, independent publishing company, in Chicago, IL in 2003. She has written seventeen books. She founded the Celebrate! Maya Project, a nonprofit youth literacy organization in July 2014, after the death of Dr. Maya Angelou.

Connect with Janis here:

Website: www.janisfkearney.com, www.celebratemayproject.org or www.rwsweekend.org

LORLETT HUDSON FRSA

MAKING THE DIFFERENCE

"If man nuh dead nuh call im duppy"

*M*eaning: You can be feeling down but don't give up on yourself - believe in yourself.

For those brought up on proverbs, this is a reminder of the stories and sayings we heard as children growing up, teaching us how to practice self-care. For those less familiar... This is a language closest to our soul and heritage passed down from generation to generation, teaching us resilience, self-leadership and survival skills. They are a source of inspiration and a laugh that still empowers and continues to shape our actions and decisions today.

I am considered instrumental in providing support to one of the most disadvantaged communities within the United Kingdom for over the last 22 years as a leadership results coach. Concerned with the growing intergenerational gap in communities, underperformance, the loss of culture and traditional support networks I created 'Things Mama Used To Say' as an innovation of Caribbean proverbs as a vital source of wisdom and a reference point for self-care and everyday skills for surviving and thriving.

Resilience is one of the principal qualities that has sustained us, and at a time when it is increasingly recognised as one of the vital ingredients of self-leadership, it is right we honor and recognise our differences and the strength we draw upon from our cultural heritage.

When I envisioned creating *'Things Mama Used to Say'* cards in 2004, many informed me that there was no market for such a product because they were too 'black'. I didn't listen to the naysayers. Thousands of copies have been sold globally. I have used these cards in my work with individuals and organizations to change perspectives, and limiting beliefs.

Proverbs are one of the best-known manifestations of Caribbean culture, with each island having their variations. They make us laugh and in truth they are a vital source of wisdom and a reference point to connect to memories, culture, community, stories and heritage.

I believe that it is important to preserve these proverbs because they were part of our upbringing handed down to the generations and we remember them with a laugh; in truth, they are part of our culture and heritage. These proverbs cards were inspired by the sayings of my grandmother who I lived with and who continues to influence my approach to community which I call 'Collective Work and Responsibility'.

I was recognized and awarded for that innovation by the Global Women Inventors and Innovators Network. I have continued to be recognized and awarded for that innovation with over 23,000 boxes of cards sold worldwide and many lives impacted since their launch in 2004.

I take a unique approach in the transplanting of wisdom of the Elders from the Caribbean and use it to nourish the contemporary community. By using a cultural heritage which is peculiar to the region, I create a bridge between our past and future potentials. I originally used the cards successfully as a tool for personal development and growth in schools across London, working exclusively with young African and Caribbean boys who had been identified as disengaged and underachieving. This was conducted in 2001, through breakfast clubs (feeding the mind and body).

I was able to facilitate changes in behaviour and subsequently affect academic achievement. The cards were ideal for use in educational settings to inspire creativity, diversity, and inclusion. They also reinforced valuable life lessons.

I believe that our communities derive their strength from the people and their relationships. In particular their willingness to work together towards a common goal. Consequently, I developed a series of coaching programs.

'One Hand Can't Clap' is a unique enterprise positively reinforcing potential and possibility in a manner echoed by President Obama in his, 'Yes We Can', presidential campaign. My work is evolving over time and evolved into a leadership retreat at my New England Private Estate in Jamaica.

There is both irony and synergy in my story and that of Edward Lorenz. Edward Lorenz was a mild-mannered meteorology professor at MIT and a lifelong New Englander who was born in 1917 in West Hartford, Connecticut.

On a winter day fifty years ago, Edward Lorenz noticed a result that would change the course of science. The unexpected result led Lorenz to a powerful insight about the way nature works.

Small changes can have large consequences. The idea came to be known as the "Butterfly Effect" after Lorenz suggested that the flap of a butterfly's wings might ultimately cause a tornado. In the 1990 movie, *Havana*, Robert Redford's character says: "a butterfly can flutter its wings over a flower in China and cause a hurricane in the Caribbean." Popular but not quite true.

The Synergy

I too noticed a small change in the individual's thinking who I had used proverbs with small shifts in perspectives led to behavior alteration which in turn led to different actions and tangible outcomes. It was these insights which led me to think of a way of creating a more tangible concept. One which captured the essence of this philosophy so that it could be shared with many more people.

I have been sent pictures of boxes of the cards from people all over the world and it has been truly humbling to have experienced the feedback from people on how the box of proverbs has impacted their lives. One card can be likened to the flap of a butterfly's wing and have an impact on the other side of the world.

The Irony

My Caribbean leadership retreat shares the namesake of the place where Edward Lorenz lived. Namely, New England. What an incredible coincidence. I evolved as a business owner over the years through this process of entrepreneurship to create a space which focuses on transformation and transition for others. Another element associated with butterflies and my place is called New England Private Estate in St Anns, Jamaica.

From a very early age, I came to know and engage with highly talented people within my community. These are not just talented people but also people with a strong entrepreneurial spirit and inspirational state of mind. I am motivated to keep this spirit alive. I support innovative possibility and act as a reminder to those who may fear losing the entrepreneurial spirit. This is what drives me now; a passion to empower people to be excited, about their lives, vision, passions, creativity, ambitions, cultural heritage, entrepreneurial spirit, and history.

Through a creative use of cultural heritage, I have embraced 'The Language of Leadership'. Doing this from a more diverse and inclusive perspective and as such leveraging the proverb quotations. This subsequently provided inspiration for the individual leadership journey.

In the lead up to the Brexit vote, many European nationals and Eastern Europeans in Britain approached me. They sought support, to deal with the impact of the xenophobia which accompanied many of the vote campaigns. These campaigns had affected their daily lives in many ways; the support provided by 'One Hand Can't Clap' was a testimony to broader inclusion and different ways of sharing the heritage of our Caribbean knowledge.

No matter the state of things before us, we can always make an impact and contribute positively to our immediate society and the world at large. I tell you this sincerely. I know this from personal experience. We can all do something and therefore, we should do something to make the world a better place no matter how little it might be.

What will you do to make a difference?

ABOUT THE AUTHOR

LORLETT HUDSON FRSA

A proven business leader, innovator and "performance maximizer" with enormous energy and vision. Her life work of over 30 years has been dedicated to building leaders, growing businesses, and advancing careers.

Lorlett is the CEO and Founder of One Hand Can't Clap, one of the UK's leading Learning and Development Enterprises. Her work with Senior African and African Caribbean leaders and entrepreneurs has produced, a powerful and substantial alumnus.

Her pioneering approach to entrepreneurship and leadership development has resulted in her winning the Silver Award of the prestigious British Female Inventors & Innovators Awards, Wavemakers National Awards, a runner up in the National Training Awards, a Member of Courvoisier The Future 500 top talents in the UK, the GLE Enterprise award and Pride of the Caribbean innovative business and brand.

She is an RSA Fellow with a network of 29,000 Fellows who want to change the world for the better. In 1754, The RSA was founded by a group of like-minded individuals to transform the world. They believe that when people come together, the possibilities are endless. She is a Cherie Blair Business Mentor and Branson Centre of Entrepreneurship Caribbean Business Mentor.

Connect with Lorlett here:

Website: Lorlett@onehandcantclap.co.uk,   www.onehandcantclap.co.uk

JESSICA BENTON

BEING WOMEN: AN APPRECIATION FOR OUR EMPOWERED SISTERHOOD

$\mathcal{I}$ have always been intrigued by 'The Butterfly Effect'. This aspect of chaos theory posits that one insignificant and inconsequential action may create a domino effect that leads towards something tremendous (positive or negative). And as humans, we are all connected to this invisible network. It tethers us to nature, the cosmos, and to one another. Therefore, a single act or intention has the potential to create a monumental impact, known and unknown.

When I was asked to participate in this anthology, I decided to focus on what it meant for us to be 'women'. This led to contemplating on how we are connected either directly or indirectly. Though our chosen paths are different and uniquely ours to follow, there exists an indescribable connection among us. This is in both our singular presence as well as the roles we choose to embrace. It is a sisterhood like no other.

Women have always been an essential part of every society. Their importance, influence, and impartation spreads across cultural, societal, political, and familial aspects of mankind. Even at the basest level, the next generation cannot be born without a woman's willingness to accept the role of mother and protector. Every culture has its own unique origin story. And in these, women are not only central, they are key game players.

Folklore, gently handed down through the eons, tells of women as goddesses, warriors, avatars and champions. In each tale, women command stages and fulfill crucial roles. Each heroine is complex; some are nurturing, caring, resilient, and willing to sacrifice themselves for the benefit of the greater good. Yet, others are ruthless, unforgiving, vengeful, and eager to mete out punishment and justice without hesitation.

Women are supremely and undisputedly powerful forces of the world. While the monomyth traditionally shines a light on the likes of King Arthur and Luke Skywalker; women, both fictional and historical, have endured, dared, and lived the cycle of known and unknown in pursuit of their destinies. It is unfortunate that these Adventuress' names do not come as readily to our lips.

Women, in turn, have not always received the recognition and acclaim so richly deserved for their contributions. With great poignancy and wisdom, Laurel Thatcher Ulrich in 1970 wrote, "well-behaved women seldom make history." Straightforward and poignant, this simple statement captures the lack of credit our illuminated sisters have received for their innovation, invention, creativity, resilience, intelligence and cultural advancement. Fifty-three years later, we still struggle, scrape and fight for the acknowledgement we deserve.

These mothers of the world are unmatched influencers. Those who chose to ride the waves of chaos and overcome uncertainty and unforeseen challenges, created order through determination and bending the world to their will. Women have touched and influenced everything from the arts to science and everything in-between; blending and manipulating the creative and analytical for the betterment of society as they envision it.

Like others, I am also linked to this amazing 'herstory'. But my story wouldn't exist without my mother. She taught me compassion, creativity, curiosity, wonder, openness, vulnerability, strength, resilience, resourcefulness, determination, and living our truth. She taught the value of carrying change courageously in our hearts and souls as I discovered my journey into adulthood. It became important to understand that positive impact requires each of us to carry the burdens of social responsibility with each step we take on our path. She gave me all these things and even so much more.

My origin story is common. My parents married before my mother finished college. Her fiancé gave his word he would always be there to take care of the family. So, a family they had; two girls about two and half years apart. One a brunette and the other a blond.

From the outside, ours appeared to be an ideal life. A new mother with two small girls managed the home while the father took care of the financial obligations of the household. But, as the axiom goes, "appearances can be deceiving". My mother had no financial freedom. She was given an "allowance" to manage shopping and other "incidentals", all at the behest of her husband. He ensured he controlled every facet of his wife's life, denying her the resources needed to properly care for the family. One day, he simply left his family for other pursuits. This one decision began a new chapter and became the epic tale of a young mother's coming of age.

A native Minnesotan, she was living alone in the deep south faced with the daunting responsibility of raising two very young daughters on her own without any means of finance or survival. She met an overwhelmed social welfare system on her own, only to be denied assistance because she owned a used car and had $750 to her name. Her circumstance was dire to say the least. She had no degree, no marketable skills, no governmental assistance, and the job she accepted only paid $1.95 per hour. Suddenly and unexpectedly, she was faced with a fork in her path - admit defeat or find the fortitude to succeed. Thankfully and with great admiration, my mother chose to fight, regardless of what obstacles life presented her. And in ways words cannot capture, she was triumphant.

Unbeknownst to the Universe, none realized the strength, savvy, resilience, resourcefulness, and determination of my heroine. She would always find a way to provide for her children. And being resolute to her the promise she made herself, failure was never an option. Through her tenacity, not only would she and her children survive, but they would thrive as well. She taught her girls the value of education, independence, self-worth, and self-reliance. Oftentimes, someone would say to her: "oh, I'm sorry to hear that your girls live in a broken home". Proudly, she would respond, "no, it was broken. I *fixed* it."

Finally, our only option to pay the bills was to sell our home. Still, my mother continued to work two jobs just to make ends meet. We embraced our "modern nomadic lifestyle" with grace and aplomb. It became our adventure as we traveled throughout Louisiana in search of a better life. Sometimes, we stayed with my mom's friends, and eventually, we moved to a rural community for 'permanent' settlement. My mother could only afford rent on a rundown trailer home but the beauty of it is that it was OURS.

The astounding thing is that my mother always transformed our challenges into fantastic exploits. In the midst of the struggles, we were introduced to exotic cuisine like tuna pâté – tuna salad served on saltines. Noodles and tomatoes became a favorite staple at the dinner table; something I still crave from time to time. My mother chose to live in the present and for the future without ever forgetting the lessons of the past.

There was only so much a single parent can endure. After years of turmoil, stress and fighting to create a safe and healthy environment for her girls, it all became too much to manage. With no viable options left, it was time to pack up and return to her midwestern roots. Our entire life barely filled a 5' x 8' U-Haul trailer. It took almost three days, but we finally reached the 'Land of 10,000 Lakes'.

Years later, I came to understand how difficult it was for my mother to ask her mother permission to return home. Their relationship was tumultuous and complicated. Nevertheless, my grandmother welcomed us without any obvious animosity.

I did not transition well to living in suburban Minnesota. During our travels, I broke my leg. I was too tall, too tom-boyish, and a socially awkward introvert that tried too hard to fit in and be liked. It didn't help that I was burdened with a thick southern drawl. My younger sister, blond and blue-eyed, blended in with the Scandinavians that had settled in the area generations ago. Her extroverted nature made her accent delightfully charming, if not beguiling. It was difficult having a sister who everyone loved. I, on the other hand, made just two friends; a boy from Iran and another boy from Peru. At least, once the cast came off, I learned to ice skate.

If living in a Minnesota suburb was challenging, nothing prepared me for our next adventure - moving to rural northwestern Wisconsin. My formative years were spent in a literal one-building school; a place where you entered kindergarten and didn't escape until you completed the 12th grade. My graduating class totaled sixty-nine students. Everyone knew everyone else's business. Most families were related, if you took the time to trace their sprawling "Family Forest". Talk about being an outsider's outsider.

As the eldest, I grew up quickly. Too quickly. I suddenly became responsible for starting dinner and ensuring chores were done before my mother got home from her long day at work. And I helped my sister with her homework. I was under tremendous pressure, but I also knew that my mother needed me. I couldn't let her down.

All of these life challenges were teaching me the amazing lessons passed from mother to daughter throughout the ages; the same survival skills she had mastered all those years ago.

When I was ready to go to college, we sat together at home and she said something I have taken to heart all these years. She told me that I could visit but I needed to know that this was no longer my home. I now belonged to the world. It would not be until I had my own child heading off to college that I fully appreciated the wisdom of her words such a long time ago.

Several years later, I married and gave birth to our only child. At times my resolve and patience were tested. But I welcomed my child's feisty spirit and champion's heart. Thankfully, with the grace of the universe, that child grew into an amazing, intelligent, thoughtful, creative, and resourceful adult.

Like my mother, I faced unexpected challenges that threatened my family's livelihood. But with my partner's support, steadfastness, and resilience, we were able to prevail against all odds. And we were also lucky enough to have loved ones who supported us during these difficult times.

My story does not only revolve around my mother and me. My legacy was to discover ways in which I could help and empower other women in different ways.

Here is an unveiling. Living in central Wisconsin, necessary change moves at a glacial speed, creating additional cultural challenges for women. Those in pursuit of their dreams and in search of the successes they desire had to do so whilst at the same time upholding obligations, responsibilities and traditions they were expected to maintain.

For over twenty years, I've worked in higher education. Every year I donated a portion of my income to the college's scholarship campaign. My contributions targeted those most in need – which traditionally were single mothers trying to create a better life for their families.

One of my mother's dreams had been to create an affordable community housing space for single parents. I could not make that happen for her. But that did not stop us from making a greater positive impact for those single mothers. Together, we created an endowed scholarship for single parents. Over the years, we have supported young mothers in need of help.

In the summer of 2021, my supervisor and I developed a three-day camp for young women called, 'Women in Industry'. The camp involved generating excitement for technology and manufacturing careers that focused on Science, Technology, Engineering and Math (STEM). These activities were introduced to young ladies, aged 12-16. Each morning, a successful local guest speaker presented on careers where women were not the norm. Each professional demonstrated that pursuing a career in a male-dominated industry was not only possible but that the only thing keeping any woman from achieving greatness - as she defined it - was her determination, innovation, and resilience. If it could be dreamed, it could be achieved.

As I conclude here, be reminded that in the ancient times of Grecian and Classical history, oracles and great beings were actually women. They advised kings, built empires and civilizations, and championed great, daring, lasting contributions to the world. Countless cultures tell of women commanding armies, navigating diplomatic waters, and overcoming unimagined feats. As with eons before, so shall women continue to irrevocably cultivate the future.

Dear great women and mothers, it is a privilege to champion a future of equity and the desired world we envision. In time, we will be recognized for our achievements and contributions. But if we do not get any, we keep on building the world we want regardless.

As we journey together in our commitment to empower our future sisters, I say unto you, "like mother, like daughter. As it has always been so shall it continue to be".

ABOUT THE AUTHOR
JESSICA BENTON

JESSICA BENTON is a 21-year veteran of higher education. Putting herself through college, she's earned a BS: Political Science & International Studies, an MS: Management and a Diversity & Inclusion advanced certificate.

She believes in life-long learning and that personal/professional growth doesn't happen in a vacuum. Her hobbies include reading, writing, fantasy shopping, painting, role-playing, playing games and spending time with her family.

Jess is purpose-driven and passionate about removing barriers that prevent people from achieving their dreams and in eliminating equity gaps for underrepresented, under-served, marginalized populations.

Her dream is to create a Positive Revolution, drawing on her sphere of like-minded colleagues to come together to create sustainable, positive, socioeconomic and political impact for future generations. Currently, she volunteers on two inclusion committees serving north central Wisconsin and is a member of Toastmasters International #972.

She lives with her husband in Wisconsin and when she isn't fantasizing about how to drive him wacky, she escapes to Netflix, Amazon Prime & Disney+.

Connect with Jessica here:

Facebook: https://www.facebook.com/jessica.benton.9003

Blogger: https://jessicabentonmsm.blogspot.com/

LinkedIn: https://www.linkedin.com/in/jessica-benton-msm/

PART VI

COMMUNITY AND SISTERHOOD, SPIRITUALITY, AND RELIGION

RITU CHOPRA

TREASURES FOUND ALONG THE WINDING ROADS

Part 1:

The Emotional Journey From Abuse To Empowerment

*L*ooking back, I realize that sometimes I followed the paths that were opened to me, and other times I paved my own. Along these paths, the stories of my life have been deeply etched on the jagged cobblestones. And each arduous turn uncovered a treasure. The gift of an opportunity to grow stronger, to be brave and to face harsh realities as they arose. I often wondered how life just slipped so quickly away. In remembering my youthful dreams for life I wondered how I got this far, walking alone along such jagged paths.

For many years I endured an unhealthy and abusive marriage. Facing threats for myself and my family. Experiencing cultural stigma, shame and fear, uncertainties, and loss of dreams that I began with, my journey was very rough but I was fortunate to have been given an education. I held a burning desire to change my life.

I was able to stop the physical abuse that often injured my spirit. The question I always asked was, 'But why?'. What does extreme abuse in a relationship achieve? Serve the ego? Control over others? Do they feel the need for this when they don't have control over their own anger, envy, insecurity or incompetence?

It leaves broken hearts, injured spirits, and damaged people. It is hardwired into some of us to lash out when we feel wronged. When someone steps on our toes, we have an overwhelming urge to step on theirs. It can be too easy to get caught up in a cycle of retaliation. A cycle of abuse that often characterizes toxic relationships. But it's not the only way to deal with conflict. We don't need to 'retaliate the 'abuse' with abuse'. But how does one find personal strength to be better than this?

In trying to find my own way, I had no one to turn to for help. The challenges I was faced with whilst experiencing abuse were at odds with my goals and dreams. They didn't fit into my vision for myself. They had no place in my ambitious future.

When those who are supposed to protect you are those who harm you, how do you reconcile this?

Believe And You Shall Find

Life can be like walking a trapeze. It's a balancing act. One that can have you walking on a tightrope with dark valleys beneath you. Often I would hear whispers that would guide me on. My faith would always lift my spirits.

I believed I could keep above the dark valleys and I aimed to reach mountain tops. I was inspired, I knew something of higher value was waiting to emerge and it always did.

Out of the darkness, bright rays of hope led me out of the winding roads and lit up the path ahead. I looked forward with hope, and maintained an attitude of optimism. In this way I was able to see the treasures of life and new ways unfolding.

As limited, mortal human beings we are sometimes unable to fully grasp the purpose of our existence. We can easily get caught up in life's drama and ignore the beautiful treasures that are presented to us. Life has a shadow side that is gloomy and dark.

But then, when you turn a corner you see glimmering snow-capped peaks of majestic & mighty mountains. It's a mesmerizing sight. High mountains inspire with their lofty heights, sparkling in the sun. They help raise me up and keep me from the gloom of the dark valleys below.

Where Do You Go From Here And Make Amends With Life?

You start from where you are standing now. Ground yourself, take a deep look at your circumstances, and ask your inner self the following.

What is my purpose in life?

What opportunities do crossroads offer me?

What do I need to do to take my journey forward?

No dark valleys could keep me down for very long. Glimmers of hope were always so bright that they pulled me up and led me on. I realized the winding roads I traveled slowly led me out of the darkness of the valleys and guided me to brighter times.

I had a nugget of inspiration from past battles that I included in my last book. *"Of all the battles I have faced, I don't know how many I've won and how many I've lost. What I remember is that I fought all of them with all my strength."* (Mastering Life, Explore Your Untapped Potential, 2008).

Never being swept far from my path, I would find myself flying high once more, smiling at new found inner strength!

I never drifted away from the sincerity, integrity, and sense of duty I was given. I performed the best I could in any difficult conditions that I found myself in. It was a roller coaster ride. But my rewards were many. Every element of my being was presented with such beautiful treasures at every turn. This included nature's beauty. The graceful movements of the waves in the ocean, awakening to gentle sounds of the wind, and seeing the majestic beauty of the mountains.

This was exactly what was happening in my life at every turn. Little treasures kept coming my way, emboldening me again and again.

I am constantly amazed. The bittersweet memories from the past seem like a single bouquet now. Only the beholder can see its beauty!

Isn't life a Divine Design? Life's experiences only serve to strengthen and wisen us.

My journey is my experience, and someone else has an equally powerful story. These stories strengthen us as individuals, families, and society through the valuable lessons pouring out of these stories. Stories are woven with courage, humility, perseverance and strength. It's important to stay strong.

I created opportunities for myself and paved my own paths many times over. I had opportunities for higher education, equality, and had ambitious dreams as a young girl. All that was snatched away from me.

I am playing my role and not backing down

At every crossroad, a new treasure opened more significant possibilities to serve humanity. Each new discovery allowed me to see the bigger picture with even bigger goals. Over the years, I observed how my story and work has inspired others to be stronger and take action for themselves.

No one will hand you a victory of any kind; you must work for it and be ready to accept the positive and the negative, the ups and downs in order to come to the final stage. Sometimes we have more strength, abilities, and drive than we acknowledge. We need to validate ourselves and find that resilience. Ignite the desire to go for it. The victory is ours to enjoy. Whether you are finding a new way to cure disease or discovering a new form of energy, every scientific breakthrough brings us one step closer to a better future for all.

As I continue to do my part to serve humanity, I see the tremendous possibilities and promise that heart-based and conscious thinking can bring. The vital energy of younger generations leads us into the future. They contribute so much to today's technological advancements and offer new promises for humanity.

However, living in the 21st Century, where civilization might be searching for signs of life in outer space, we still need to work on making life equal for our people in our homes, families, communities, and societies. Respect for each other regardless of gender is simply a human right.

I hope every reader will find their passion, creativity, and desire to bring changes to keep our planet beautiful, our nations, societies, communities, and families healthy and happy.

Part 2:

From Abuse to Advocacy And Equity for All

We can agree on women and girls' empowerment and equal rights. Are these rights actually given and are all women fairly treated? Each culture or community has its own definition of women's empowerment.

There is a myriad of ways to look at the issue of empowerment. I find that everyone needs empowerment, both men and women. An attitude of equality should not be limited to women. Each and every member of society must treat one another with equality, respect and as valuable human beings.

Women have contributed to their economies through the centuries, from agriculture to aerospace. Women in many developing countries have led initiatives to reform societies from barriers that limit the growth process, dignity and empowerment. Often these are seen as collective efforts backed by political powers to implement these changes. Despite the growth in many sectors to provide women with more opportunities in the 21st Century than ever, there are interesting dynamics when it comes to women playing dual roles, seeking recognition, and proving their worth.

I find that the gender roles and subconscious conditioning from centuries of patterns are still evident in our behaviors. Regardless of education levels, skills, and capabilities to deliver, the perceptions and gender 'bias' are not uncommon. With all good intentions, this is still a problem for many women to communicate effectively without being misunderstood, combative, aggressive, or disregarded.

The pre-pandemic world we knew about two years ago has changed and so have our needs as families, businesses, organizations, and economic design. In the next few decades, humanity will face many challenges even if we try to mitigate the damage we've done to the planet. The current ecosystems demand many changes, and the future will face multifold challenges in the next few decades. By the mid-21st Century, the predictions indicate humanitarian challenges, including environmental, climate, food, and drinking water shortages in many parts of the world, future pandemics, or warfare. As we get closer to the mid-century, the best way is to take action now. PERIOD.

Sustainable earth and solid economic foundations need collaborative effort. It will be daunting, but we must face it if we want to protect our planet for future generations. Eco-systems all over the world are under immense pressure. The loss of biodiversity, pollution of our oceans, future pandemics, or even warfare cannot be ignored. It may seem difficult to change the course of the future of our planet, but we do have the power to do so and create a sustainable healthy planet and equality of life for its habitants.

ABOUT THE AUTHOR
RITU CHOPRA

RITU CHOPRA inspires people with her coaching sincerity and professional leadership experience that includes managing business and IT operations for 25 years. She employs her management and coaching expertise to lead corporate teams, helping to resolve conflicts between IT and non-IT business partners, increase employee engagement, and empower everyone she works with.

As president of Chopra Management Services, Ritu is a creative force, motivational speaker, and certified leadership coach with personal projects, she is committed to giving back to the community. She wrote '*Art of Life*' and '*Mastering Life*', focusing on personal mastery for professional success. Her upcoming titles are '*Women Leadership in the 21st Century*' and '*Magic in Mindfulness*'.

Ritu hosts and executive produces 'Despite the Challenges®,' a TV show about people who overcome impending circumstances, disabilities, or other barriers to contribute to society. She is founder of 'Lead My Way', a Domestic Violence Advocacy NGO and has lived her life adopting her eastern philosophies and uses her global business methodologies, management skills and tools gained through her career with Fortune 500 Companies in her Management Consulting practices.

Connect with Ritu here:

Website: www.RituChopra.com

LinkedIn: https://www.LinkedIn.com/in/RituGChopra

Instagram: https://www.instagram.com/coachrituchopra/

TABITA MANGOAELA

FOLLOW THE SACRED PATH

T hose who live with a sense of the sacred are constantly aware

that *"there is more to life than what we see on the surface"*. Kate Turlington wrote that. By knowing this, it brings a mystical dimension into one's life as well as connecting to the very source or essence of life.

Those who revere the sacred are often observed to be more at peace with life. In African countries people honor what is sacred to a tribe or nation. Using their spiritual consciousness, they prioritize many different sacred practices. Whilst this has been established as common knowledge, much still needs to be done to help others to reach this state of consciousness.

Africa is a continent with so much diversity, rich in history and culture. There are also many pressing issues and challenges facing its people. In one way or the other, we as Africans are always affected by these shortcomings. To improve things takes action both individually and collectively.

Lesotho is an interesting case study. It demonstrates the dilemma many are faced with using modern but failing systems across Africa. Lesotho is a small kingdom in Southern Africa that is completely landlocked by South Africa. It is one of the poorest countries in the world yet has an abundance of diamonds and a massive water supply. Rivers in Lesotho are called 'White Gold' because they provide water for hydro-electrical plants that serve Lesotho as well as South Africa, Botswana, and Namibia. The natural beauty of the river system further serves as a vital resource in the eco-tourism sector.

Africa has also witnessed the deliberate disruption of Mother Earth that in turn comes back to haunt us.

When I met my late partner, Teboho Matete, in 2015, I was surprised that he advocated against the construction of more dams in the mountains. As an environmental justice advocate, he argued that mountain ecosystems are not designed to be altered by engineering projects. This is because it involves building tarred roads, relocating whole villages, tunneling through mountains and releasing water catchments that were never meant to be brought to the surface.

Underground streams and hidden lakes below the earth's crust feed springs that provide the purest Natural Spring Water in the world. Numerous natural wells supply clean water to villages. In addition to this, the droplets of water seep through the obsidian rock of certain cliffs, forming icicles in winter that become crystallized. Then the icicles fuse with obsidian and create a crystal called *mahakoe [pronounced mahakway]*.

As a small child, I was fascinated by these crystals. Whenever my family went for a day's excursion in the highlands we explored the majestic country. I loved its blue mountains, wide open spaces, and winding rivers.

There is a silence in the mountains that invites you to pause and to suspend day-to-day cares and concerns. It inspires one to ponder how small we humans are in the universal scheme of creation.

Therefore, it is sad to see the essence of the earth, nature and good holdings being destroyed before our very eyes. These alterations and disruptions in one way or another pose disastrous threats to mankind. In line with this, Teboho argued consistently that a lot of developments that have taken place across Africa are not in fact sustainable. This is due to many key factors not always being taken into consideration regarding the environment.

One of the most important lessons in my journey has been that of becoming self-grounded. As writers tend to live inside their heads, and as someone who leans strongly towards the mystical dimension of nature, I easily got lost in my inner world and struggled to find the right form of self-expression. On long morning walks at dawn or hikes across the hills, Teboho showed me how self-grounding practices allow the stream of consciousness to inform whatever work we do.

Spending time in nature is a form of escape from the realities of the world below. It serves as a time-out to renew one's mind and refresh the spirit.

Nature is a sacred space in which to commune with God and my own higher self.

Illustration: Recycled Art from Bottle Caps collected over a 3-month period in 2017

In the process of self-awareness and through the help of Teboho, I have explored both my inner and outer worlds. Through the morning walking and hiking on great mountains, I have been able to capture and understand the mystical and sacred dimensions and paths of my life.

I have taken to writing poetry and the short pieces of prose have a healing motif in them. The process of writing in itself has been a channel for accessing the essence of life. My writings focus on the sacred paths and dimensions of life.

As a conscious being in the sacred path and dimension of life, I have become more of a mystic and inner self-conscious being. This has further evolved and birthed mystical poems and creative literary pieces. And has helped my freelance writing career.

In his tireless effort to help and lead me into my own sacred path, Teboho introduced me to an artist called Tereo. She makes crafts from recyclable materials and runs a series of workshops for artisans called *Craft Your Path.* Partnering with her company and brand, Madhouse Rain, we created a recycled art project. This was to serve as the springboard for a long-term community-based organization project called Metro Green.

Over four years, I designed project plans and blueprints for the construction of a bio-gas plant. This included workshop evaluations and the U.N.D.P Waste Analysis Model. This is outlined in a white paper *'On Creating A Circular Green Economy In Lesotho'* (copyright 2021).

Intellectuals told me they were impressed by the projects' concept. Donor agencies were interested but did not have the resources to fund such a huge project. Private sector companies were skeptical that investing in such an undertaking would yield dividends. International development agencies were curious about how we had come up with an entire country's plan all on our own, having no affiliation with any environmental agency or body except the almost defunct United Nations Environment Program in Lesotho.

"Isn't Lesotho already green?", an advisor to the City Mayor asked. That forced us to stop and think. Depending on what criteria are used in defining a green country, the mayor's advisor had a point. Lesotho may not have the renewable energy infrastructure, technologies, and economic outputs that make a country green, but it does have enormous potential to produce clean energy that could facilitate the switch to a circular green economy.

All of these topics were trending in think-tanks in 2019 but nothing was done on the ground to translate the vision of a Green Country Plan into practical strategies and climate action. These aspirations failed for lack of support and adequate funding.

When Teboho passed away I gradually moved away from the practices we had shared for seven years. This is buried in the fact that the sacred path we had been walking and working on together came to an end in an unexpected mudslide coming down from the hills.

Earlier, he had warned about this being possible due to the disruption of the environment. But no one gave attention to anything that he said. As discouraging as it is, I will continue to build on the legacy that Teboho left behind, especially that of the Green Kingdom initiative.

While I weep over the loss of everything Teboho and I tirelessly worked towards, not everything has gone down the drain. The situation gave birth to a gift to humanity which is vividly engraved in my poetic and prosaic pieces. These remind everyone of the importance of honoring the sacred paths and requirements of our lives.

As complicated as this all may appear, my life has been complicated too. I haven't always found it simple to follow the sacred path. Teboho tried bringing the land back into sacred respect. He took me in and then hurriedly left. In my grief, I tried making sense from this. The path seemed to be lost, thereby doubling my grief of losing him. I missed all that he stood for and wanted for this impoverished land.

The discourse of following the sacred path is beyond Teboho and I. It is beyond the length and breadth of Lesotho. It is a natural gift that abounds with power that could be good for this impoverished state.

Following the sacred path is beyond the cultures and sacredness of the African continent. It means doing right by the disruptions of the African landscapes. It involves changing the way we are ripping off the African continent, endangering the landscape for its inhabitants.

We must stop consciously and unconsciously creating natural dangers for Africans and others in the world.

Speaking about following the sacred path is an endless commitment. In order for it to achieve outcomes requires a focus that is birthed to bring a healthy and reviving consciousness. Individually, collectively, and as a nation and continent, all Africans need to follow the sacred path.

For practical ways to follow a sacred path, follow my blog 'Our Green Kingdom' or explore resources offered on my author's website, Tabrizi. They will go live in March 2023.

The message in all of my writing, informed by all that I learned from Teboho and Tereo, is that Africans need to return to indigenous knowledge and practices. Once we do this and share a natural way of living and being that honors the sacredness of the earth and of the human experience, the so-called developed, Westernized nations that imposed their civilizations on other parts of the world, will realize that a country like Lesotho never being developed was actually a blessing.

ABOUT THE AUTHOR
TABITA MANGOAELA

TABITA MANGOAELA is a first-time author from Lesotho who spent many years traveling on the African continent learning about its arts and culture.

She returned permanently to Lesotho in 2010 after a 15-year consulting career in South Africa, where she was associated with organizational development consultancies. In Lesotho, she worked as a technical and grant writer, assisting civil society organizations in attracting funding. She also worked with her church to develop content for youth programs and empowerment projects. She was the ghostwriter for Leonard Makhoane's book, *Systems Failed, Time To Come Full Circle* that he self-published in 2012.

In 2015, Tabita began working full-time with Metro Green Art. This cooperative taught youth to recover recyclable materials and produce recycled art. Over a seven-year period, Tabita devoted her expertise to growing these projects and casting the vision of a Green Kingdom Country Plan. The Cooperative was deregistered after their CEO passed away in 2022. Tabita now works full-time as a content writer and author of Creative Nonfiction pieces about African culture.

Connect with Tabitha here:

https://www.linkedin.com/in/tabita-mangoaela-b69a27232/

SAMANTHA LOUISE

THE GOLDEN THREAD OF WHIMSICAL WISDOM

Through the ages, women have led change to improve the lives of

the generations yet to be born. The nature of womanhood inherently connects with our ancestors. We link arms and walk together as warriors of love, growth, and equity. Although we can at times be isolated, ostracized, disrespected, or even killed, we still embrace a powerful spirit. We have a fiery compassion that can rewrite the unwritten rules of cultural injustice.

We continue to develop and improve inhumane societal norms to make life better for the collective. How is it that women do these things? What causes the wonderful ripple effect to pass on skills and knowledge that nurture growth and transformation? What are the wisdoms we share in our families, communities, and organizations?

Women create and live vibrant legacies via golden threads, linked in our sisterhood. Whimsical wisdom is shared through the secret codes of womanhood. This naturally occurs as we carry out roles as advocates and warriors, fighting for an evolved human experience. Woven into the fabric of each compassionate change agent, is an unapologetic commitment to rebel against wrongdoings. We heal and nurture in order to provide wellbeing. We also provide growth and personal development through teaching balance, discernment, and new perspectives. As powerful influencers we achieve many things via fearless individuation, courageous community organizing, and meaningful mentorships.

As a pointed needle weaves strong thread through the fabric of a quilt, so does the quest for justice and equality create a stronghold among girls and women. The combination of vibrant colors, unique textures, and the intricate material of each creates a kaleidoscope of beauty. Reflective of the symphony of voices and diverse experiences lived by the women who thoughtfully navigate the stories that shape their future.

A Beautiful Soul Is Born - Ignite Your Imagination

The world's greatest gifts, often hidden in the smallest form, are delivered with the potential of excellence embedded within. When she is newly born she doesn't yet know what lies ahead on her journey. Her wondrous journey through life is yet to unfold.

How does she come to her mark in this magnificent world? She does this by her very nature, from the very fiber of her being. This girl is to be nurtured by the forest, cleansed by water, inspired by the wind, focused like fire, and become solid like stone. Watch her grow.

Brave Girl, Love Yourself Fiercely

The lesson of self-love is the most important first step. Then to live a life guided by her heart's desires. Nourished by the essence of nature, her inherent values will guide the intent of her actions. She is born out of purity and grace and endures with power and grit.

During childhood, her explorations of the wild teach her about compassion for animals, patience with plants and utilizing the imagination of universal design. In quiet solitude solace is found from connection with her source. By her teenage years she believed life could not get any better. Nothing can stand in her way because she is invincible.

While the world around her continues to turn, she develops a hope like fire deep within her soul to guide every step she takes. Her physical body takes a new form - womanhood. Her mind expands with new information daily, and her soul remains steadfast in its conviction to be true to herself.

Daughter of Joy, Voice Your Needs

Oddly, what she knows about life and that still small voice within her, begins to be challenged. Episodes of confusion overwhelm her awesome mind. Dis-ease enters her beautiful body, and holds captive the voice of freedom and love. What the world needs so badly is now tucked away, hidden from anyone that might tease, disrupt, or destroy the whimsical ideas of the girl.

No longer does she believe that her voice matters. Without permission to freely express self, she retreats underground.

In stealth mode, she begins to visualize the woman she must become in order to reclaim her lost and stolen power. But who is she destined to become? What visionary transformation will be realized and created by her hands alone? She is designed for the kind of change that heals the hurts of ancestral generations before her, and inspires the hearts of future followers.

Firstly, she must restore control of her own life. Take back her personal power, and develop strength of voice. Then she can live by her own personal agency and from this place of power she can help others to do the same.

Warrior Heart, Go Lead the Healing of Self And of Your Community

The young woman plans her next move to make the lives of her neighbors and community members better. She has a vision of grandeur to reach far and wide, cultivating roots of love as she leads change.

Will they accept the vision? Only if their voice is echoed in the plan. How will she establish trust? Where will she begin? Her questions are endless. The self-doubt dances around her mind. Seducing her to quit and simply walk away from her dreams. She is tempted to abandon her inner knowing - just to end the endless questioning and self sabotage. But the intuition that wakes her soul every day wins through. Finally reacquainted with her inherent wisdom, she is once more confident. She is determined to reconcile disharmony among people. She knows this is her calling and destiny.

Strong Woman, Know Your Worth

She continues despite the world constantly questioning her methods. The woman playfully dodges the sideways glances and odd looks people shoot at her as she passes them on the street.

Not all people will fully understand that her heart is designed to serve, to give, to love. However, comfort is found in constancy and the values of her community. She finds the powerful morals, ethics, and values rooted in her own community are the foundation to catalyze future work.

Her passion grows each day as she recognizes the need for her unique skills. Others are not listening; the people's needs are not being heard by anyone else. She finds ways to build bonds. Breaking bread, building relationships and trust in precious and vulnerable moments.

Imagining innovations together with others. New systems can be designed through the unification of diverse ideas. Taking action now. Leaping beyond the words and plans and faithfully moving forward towards tangible results.

Smart, nerdy, unique, and quirky are no longer labels of ignorant judgment. The recontextualized embodiment is now procured in words such as strategic, precise, savvy, and innovative leader.

Guardian of Light, Live your Vision

Maturity. No more preaching. No more complaining. Rather than becoming stuffy and bland, sophistication calls her back inside of herself. She experiences a reconnection of mind, body, and soul once again. Spending hours in quietude she listens to her heart, regains the trust of her intuition, and steps into her greatness.

With enormous responsibility placed in her hands, she rises to the occasion. She is confident she can keep moving towards the ultimate goal. A life of serenity, peace, and clarity. But what about others? The safeguards of habit, logic, and personal boundaries create a safety that some do not wish to move from. Feeling a deep sense of security, the woman surrenders all intentions, thoughts, and feelings to create space for a new genius to emerge. In a vision, she sees it clearly, a life of cooperation, tranquility, and unity.

Mother of Might, Leave Your Legacy of Love

As a wise woman, she now reflects on her walk through life. Giddy with the satisfaction of the love and wisdom she has imparted on the world. She smiles as God's wink shines upon her. The woman has done well.

She acknowledges the valleys she navigated, and the mountains she climbed. Proud of herself for the demons she has slayed. Although the world is still craving the cure for pain and suffering, she is pleased with her efforts. The wise woman is content and at peace with a life that has been full of service and meaning. Who could ask for more? What else is there to give?

Giver of Life, Inspire Courageous Actions

She never stops or turns back. Her heart refuses to give in to the guilt from mistakes of the past. A satisfied mind of positive plans united with an everlasting soul of vitality. She is ready for yet another adventure. With added enthusiasm, the woman again makes known her plans of unending support for change.

She no longer commands attention as the leader out front. This time, she inspires radical vision and plants seeds of hope among women like her former self. She supports them while they are facing their fears to voice their opinions. Many women have been feeling alone in the fight for self-worth. But now, each new connection is an opportunity to change yet another life towards greatness. Their influence in the world will ripple the blessings of sisterhood as hers does. Directly from the heart, across the world for eternity.

Spirit of Kindness, Grow Positive Change

Finally, the quest is complete. The exhausting battle is over. She has transformed from fighter to nurturer by becoming a learned soul. She is truly a wise woman now. No more does she contribute to the hurt of people. Instead, her path is set on inspiring peaceful and positive change. Where tired souls are born anew. Where weary hearts are relieved of fear and filled with love.

It is in this space intentionally created for the future, that she invites fellow seekers, light bearers and healers. Her truth in the world acts like a boomerang. Her community responds and beckons for more wisdom to be shared.

Feeling their invitation, she grins and the mischievous twinkle in her eyes from girlhood is back. With open arms and an open heart she gestures to the girls and women around her. All are embraced in her knowledge and love. Here, she presents to the world, generations of whimsical wisdom that is woven together with trust and an unbreakable golden thread.

These mystical threads of feminine leadership require fierce compassion and understanding. So much destruction is rampant in our world today. With knowledge of the best and the worst of human experience this can teach patience and assist in defining boundaries in managing to live amongst it. The women learn to preserve wellness, eliminate suffering, and thrive. It all begins with love. Love is a grounding place for validation and knowing one's worth and value. This supports courageous thought and action.

This model results in authentic individuation and self-discovery. Integrated into the collective, this model results in a paradigm shift, communal healing, and justice.

The imperative to revive cultural storytelling and reinvigorate intergenerational collaboration establishes the foundations of what women have lived and died for through the ages. This is a marriage of intuition and logic. It replaces mechanical systems of inequity with ecosystems of developmentally appropriate experiences. It provides hands-on learning, and the blossoming of a soul destined to positively change the world.

The whimsical wisdom of women has been oppressed, stolen, and destroyed. Yet, it remains alive and well in souls worldwide. Epigenetic transfer? Perhaps. Coded within our DNA? Maybe. Inherent in our nature? I believe so.

Please, slow down sisters. The rush of our world can sweep us away from its chaos and noise. Reclaim the inner voice of wisdom passed on to empower you.

As a special Child, Mother, Friend, Sister, Companion, Warrior, Visionary, Architect, Lover, Creator, and Nurturer, you will find all that you need within yourself. It is there at any given moment. The true challenge is accepting your gift of greatness and creating space for other girls and women to do the same.

You are a woman woven from the same fabric of my ancestors. You have your own ancestral power. Nothing is too big for you to overcome. Together, let's rise. It is time to change the world and make it a better place by weaving our whimsical wisdom day by day. Together we create an artistic masterpiece in the fabric of life. Woven with the mystical golden thread that binds us in our eternally powerful and potent sisterhood.

ABOUT THE AUTHOR
SAMANTHA LOUISE

SAMANTHA LOUISE is a leadership cultivator guiding girls and young women to reclaim their personal power as natural born leaders. She is an author, a Minnesota Teacher of the Year, and holds a Master's degree in Educational Leadership. Her approach to leadership and learning offers hands-on experiences to develop selfhood for self-leadership, sisterhood for healthy relationships, and leaderhood to inspire change in the world around us.

Every experience designed by Samantha incorporates whole person wellbeing, cultural mindbody science, and interfaith spiritual practices. Golden Threads of Whimsical Wisdom is a poetic expression of the sense-making and developmental processes of Samantha Louise from girlhood and teenhood into womanhood.

Samantha has been featured on such popular podcasts as *She's Invincible, The Influential Woman*, and *The Rhonda Grant Show* to discuss demasculinizing women, healing through vulnerable justice, and new perspectives on leadership. From a farm in rural America, Samantha is a small-town girl with a world-wide vision to transform leadership development and personal empowerment for next generation female leaders from every corner of the globe.

Connect with Samantha here:

Website: samanthalouise.co

Email: grow@samanthalouise.co

More: linktr.ee/samanthalouise.co

Made in the USA
Monee, IL
03 May 2023